Texas Mexican Americans and Postwar Civil Rights

[MAGGIE RIVAS-RODRIGUEZ]

Texas Mexican Americans and Postwar Civil Rights

University of Texas Press ⌇ AUSTIN

Requests for permission to reproduce material from this work should be sent
to:
    Permissions
    University of Texas Press
    P.O. Box 7819
    Austin, TX 78713-7819
    http://utpress.utexas.edu/index.php/rp-form
♾ The paper used in this book meets the minimum requirements of ANSI/NISO
Z39.48-1992 (R1997) (Permanence of Paper).

LIBRARY OF CONGRESS CATALOGING-IN-PUBLICATION DATA

Rivas-Rodriguez, Maggie, author.
    Texas Mexican Americans and postwar civil rights /
Maggie Rivas-Rodriguez. — First edition.
        pages   cm
    Includes bibliographical references and index.
        ISBN 978-0-292-76751-5 (cloth : alk. paper) — ISBN 978-0-292-76752-2
(pbk. : alk. paper) — ISBN 978-0-292-76754-6 (library e-book) —
ISBN 978-0-292-76753-9 (non-library e-book)
1. Mexican Americans—Civil rights—Texas.   2. School integration—
Texas—Alpine.   3. Discrimination in employment—Texas—El Paso.
4. Police—Employment—Texas—El Paso.   5. Mexican American Legal
Defense and Educational Fund—History.   6. Race discrimination—Texas.
7. Texas—Race relations.   I. Title.
    F395.M5R528   2015
    323.1168′72073—dc23   2014046111

doi:10.7560/767515

To the World War II–era civil rights warhorses

Contents

Preface

In 1992, MALDEF was in the middle of a long-running class-action lawsuit against the state of Texas and its two flagship universities: the University of Texas at Austin and Texas A&M University. The suit, LULAC et al. v. Richards et al., alleged that the state concentrated its higher-education wealth on the flagship campuses at the expense of the colleges and universities on the Texas-Mexico border. (Although the case would be decided in favor of the state, the lawsuit led to large-scale improvements in the allocation of funds and would create several affiliations with both the Texas A&M system and the University of Texas system.) At the time, I was a reporter, covering the U.S.-Mexico border for the *Dallas Morning News* and staying abreast of LULAC et al. v. Richards. As journalists do, I was writing a "takeout"—a story that explores some aspect of a larger issue, a device often used to stay current with a major ongoing story. That takeout was a profile of MALDEF; an interview with the attorney Pete Tijerina was part of the story.

As we sat in his San Antonio office, Tijerina told me about the early days of the organization. At the close of the interview, Tijerina mentioned that he was a veteran of World War II, as was my own father. "*All us old civil rights warhorses are World War II vets*," Tijerina said.

That offhand comment led me to write another story about the Mexican American World War II generation and civil rights. My article, "Brothers in Arms," ran as the cover story of the now-defunct *Dallas Morning News*'s Sunday magazine for December 6, 1992, and the piece would inspire what has become the Voces Oral History Project.

In the course of reporting that longer story in 1992, I became aware of the dearth of literature on the Mexican American WWII civil rights work. This volume, then, has its roots in those 1992 interviews with Pete Tijerina, Albert Armendariz of El Paso, Pete and Elena Gallego of Alpine, and others. Tijerina helped me understand the early days of MALDEF; Armendariz explained how another World War II–era veteran, Raymond Telles, opened the ranks of the police and fire departments; and Pete and Elena Gallego explained the steps they and their West Texas community took to integrate their schools. Those three stories, emerging from the reporting for the 1992 magazine article, make up the three chapters of this book. The story has now come full circle.

This book is divided into two parts. The first part consists of two chapters on local civil rights efforts. The Alpine chapter is self-contained, focusing on the history of Alpine's multistep and independent struggle to create a single school for all its students: Mexican American, African American, and white. There was ample material to use: the local newspaper, the *Alpine Avalanche*, covered the struggle in depth, and there were participants involved who could be interviewed for both the facts and the flavor of the times. There was also solid archival material to build on at the state archives, as well as at the Sul Ross State University library. Beyond those primary sources, there was substantial secondary literature to consult on the integration of schools in Texas.

A note on the Alpine chapter: I chose to use long quotations to preserve the flow of the interviews, in particular the switching between English and Spanish. I hope the reader will agree with me that the long quotes contribute to the understanding of what was at issue in that West Texas community.

The second chapter, on the integration of the police department in El Paso, was more problematic from a research standpoint because efforts to integrate the department have not been as fully researched. Records from the City of El Paso were incomplete and efforts to integrate the civil service rank went unnoticed by local news media. It is perhaps not surprising that the integration had not been fully chronicled by local journalists: it was largely a bureaucratic story of civil service commissions and occasional lawsuits that are not as obvious as, say, a press conference. This chapter relied heavily on oral interviews, verifying information with other sources where possible. I hope that some of the material revealed here will pique the interest of other researchers to explore this topic and to extend its study to other cities throughout the country.

Finally, the MALDEF chapter is the most extensive, as there were numerous archives and several relevant secondary sources to consult. There were also helpful oral history interviews conducted by formal oral history projects and by individual scholars who were kind enough to share them.

There has been some research on MALDEF, some of which is cited in that chapter. But as the legal scholar Michael Olivas has lamented, there has not yet been a book-length treatment of this important civil rights organization. This chapter is not that book; it revolves only around the creation and first two years of MALDEF, and it is not an evaluation of the cases involved. Instead, it provides the first detailed explication of the many personalities and events involved during those early attempts at establishing a litigation arm of the Mexican American civil rights movement.

This narrative about the three civil rights efforts is intended to shed light on the stories behind the headlines or, in some cases, the headlines that never were. I hope this work engenders a better appreciation of the many steps required to bring about greater equality for Mexican Americans in Texas and beyond.

Acknowledgments

Many have had a part in the creation of this book. To name but a few:

Thank you to the many men and women who patiently participated in interviews with the U.S. Latino & Latina WWII Oral History Project, now called the Voces Oral History Project. This includes the interviewers, sometimes college students and other times outside volunteers. I include in this volume only a handful of the many interviews that have helped me to understand the times. I hope our interview subjects and interviewers read these accounts and will understand our request for so much detail in the interviews. A special thanks to Leo Dominguez, of Alpine, for going above and beyond, helping us find photographs and people to interview.

At the University of Texas at Austin, I am fortunate to have a large family to lean on. The Center for Mexican American Studies (CMAS) at UT-Austin provided me with a semester leave in fall 2011 to help with work on this book. CMAS also hosted a research presentation so that I could relate findings and receive responses that also helped focus my approach. To CMAS, director Dominó Perez and associate director Nicole Guidotti-Hernández, and the rest of the dedicated CMAS staff and family: thank you.

As always, thank you to my home department in journalism. Our administrative staff, particularly Janice Henderson and Lourdes Jones, responded to requests small and large in order to "make things happen" for me and for the Voces Oral History Project. And thank you to our former department chair, Glenn Frankel, who has been a committed champion of my work.

Tino Mauricio, the brilliant photographer and photo editor at Voces, took care of all our photographic needs. Nicole Cruz, the efficient program coordinator at Voces, found herself roped into many more small chores than she should have expected when she started working with me in 2013. Thank you to these two stalwarts.

UT's Moody College of Communication, home to the School of Journalism where I teach, has shared its many resources with our project, enabling me and the Voces Oral History Project to do our work. Thank you especially to Dean Rod Hart, who has supported public symposia and conferences; R. T. Fehlhafer, in human resources; Jeff Toreki, in accounting; Jay Whitman, grants specialist. And our many, many friends on the technology team, led by Charles Soto: Scott Calhoun, Larry Horvat, Khaled Jaber, Kamran Hooshmand, Dipto Chaudhuri, David Cox, Rod Edwards, Brian Parrett, Dave Wiginton, Efraín Colón-Cabrera, Jeff Fromme, Mark Rogers, Josh Kinney, Annelle Harris, and John Kimbrough. They have provided technical advice, training, equipment check-out, and fixes. We simply couldn't do our work without them.

There have been many outside Austin who helped: Mariana Cristancho-Ahn, a master's student at the Columbia Graduate School of Journalism in the fall 2010, who visited the Ford Foundation archives in New York and download voluminous records for my use. Mary L. Holguín at the El Paso City Hall was my contact who procured for me from storage dozens of boxes with Civil Service Commission and City Council records. My brother Robert "Bobby" Rivas in El Paso has helped me by making photocopies of some El Paso municipal records. (After calling on him so many times for other research-related requests since 1999, mostly doing interviews, he now protests a bit. But he still complies.)

The librarians at Sul Ross State University in Alpine have been helpful to our project for years, especially B. J. Gallego and Melleta Bell. Many thanks for their resourcefulness and alacrity in responding to our many requests.

A few colleagues gave insightful reviews early on: Al Kauffman, now a law professor at St. Mary's Law School in San Antonio, and a former MALDEF staff attorney, read through an early version of the MALDEF chapter and made insightful suggestions. Guadalupe San Miguel, a history professor at the University of Houston, provided important recommendations that greatly improved the Alpine chapter. My former department chair, Glenn Frankel, also read selections and offered a useful critique.

UC–Santa Barbara Professor Mario T. García was kind enough to share his interviews of former El Paso Mayor Raymond Telles and Albert Armendariz with me. I must also thank him for documenting so much of Mexican American and El Paso history, thus providing the secondary resources that have made my work more doable than it would have been otherwise.

Thank you to the close reading by the publisher's reviewers, who also helped to shape this final product.

And of course, Theresa May, a dream of an editor, deserves credit for her gentle recommendations and calm and sure hand in making sure all was going according to schedule.

My husband, Gil, is my immensely patient and drama-free technical adviser at home. He knows what to do when the footnote program, or any computer function, goes awry. He also listens to me, is interested in my work, and asks good questions. Most important, his love sustains me in ways large and small.

Finally, my two teenage sons, Ramón and Agustín, long-standing volunteers, have accompanied me on research trips to Alpine and throughout the country (I personally pay their way, thank you very much). They have scanned photos, set up/taken down equipment, and helped with whatever needed to be done. My heart soars when I watch them work because I know the exciting possibilities that await them. I am reminded that those opportunities did not come easily: they were made available by the generations that have gone before. I also know that their generation must also pick up the torch, in whatever way they can. I hope we have prepared them well.

Texas Mexican Americans and Postwar Civil Rights

Introduction

In 1968, the U.S. Commission on Civil Rights held a five-day hearing in San Antonio on the civil rights problems of the Mexican American people in the five southwestern states. In the 757-page transcript of the hearing—and another 491 pages of exhibits—witnesses detailed instances of police abuse, grand jury exclusion of Mexican Americans, unequal educational and employment opportunities, and political underrepresentation. One speaker, a Native American scholar who was an authority on educational obstacles facing Mexican American students, attributed low educational attainment to "the problems of alienation and especially powerlessness . . . , [which are] the result of the Mexican conquest."[1]

Many of the witnesses noted the widespread powerlessness of the Mexican American community: the inequality was woven into the system, making it difficult, if not impossible, to isolate, for instance, the lack of Mexican American political representation from voting rights, educational opportunities, and so on.

Yet even while Mexican Americans faced tremendous oppression, there were thriving communities, home to Spanish- and English-language newspapers that covered them, artists, musicians, businesses, churches, and families that demonstrated tremendous resourcefulness in overcoming the daily adversities. Despite the pervasive inequality, the Mexican American people persevered, resisting and making gains as possible.

Undoubtedly, Mexican Americans' standing as "strangers in their own land," could be traced to the Mexican-American War, 1846–1848. The United States had provoked the war in a brazen attempt to fulfill its Manifest Destiny—"a continental nation with harbors on the Pacific," as one historian put it.[2] For $15 million, Mexico lost—some would say was robbed of—its claim to the area that consists of present-day New Mexico, Arizona, California, Nevada, and parts of Colorado, Arizona, Utah, and Oklahoma.[3] The Treaty of Guadalupe Hidalgo (1848), which ended the U.S.-Mexico War, guaranteed the Mexicans who chose to stay in what would now be U.S. territory would be "incorporated into the Union of the United States, and . . . be admitted at the proper time (to be judged by the Congress of the United States) to the enjoyment of all rights of citizens of the United States." This was stated in Article IX of the Treaty of Guadalupe Hidalgo. Montejano writes that the popular opinion of the time (except for some dissent in the Northeast) expressed a united belief that Mexicans were not ready for an "equal union" with Americans, and some senators, like John C. Calhoun, argued that they never would be.[4] Indeed, land rights were violated, sometimes with the collusion of law enforcement agents. Laws were eventually passed outlawing the use of foreign languages, including Spanish, on public school grounds, and children were punished if they disobeyed. Schools were segregated. In many rural communities, there were no schools for the Mexican American children past fourth grade, or in other cases, eighth grade. Police brutality was commonplace; political representation was scant. Many jobs, including those well-paying civil service positions, were off-limits to Spanish-surnamed applicants. And if Mexican Americans wished to pursue justice through the courts, the cost of legal battles was prohibitive. Once a case could be pressed, plaintiffs were stymied by juries that generally excluded Mexican Americans.[5] In a few cases, wealthy Mexican Americans participated within the dominant society and came to hold appointed, or even elected, office. Where they could, those elite Mexican Americans worked to improve conditions for all Mexican Americans.[6]

Mexican Americans resisted as they could, facing violence and intimidation. Organizations were founded for greater protection. From the late 1800s and to the 1930s, the groups went about quietly fomenting change within "the often-hostile environment of Anglo-America," writes Julie Pycior.[7] Spanish-language newspapers carried information about events and the issues facing the Mexican American community, but English-language newspapers rarely noted the presence or activities of Mexican Americans. Early organizations advocated for Mexican American rights in Texas, but none could sustain a prolonged or very effective assault on the pervasive discrimination. The resistance wasn't limited to Texas, of course. In New Mexico, *juntas de indignación* were meetings held to challenge a variety of grievances: racist stereotyping, unfair political actions, and even "a bad parish priest," writes Phillip Gonzales. In some cases, organizations grew out of the meetings.[8] In Arizona, there were mutual-aid societies to observe Mexican holidays. And in Tucson, Arizona, the Alianza Hispana Americana sprang up in 1894 to counter the anti-immigrant fervor that gripped the state.[9] Similarly, Mexican Americans in California, having lost their land and political power by the 1880s, also formed political and cultural clubs, as well as *"juntas patrióticas,"* which organized Mexican holidays.[10]

Perhaps the one early organization that was the closest model for the Mexican American Legal Defense and Educational Fund was the Liga Protectora Mexicana, begun in San Antonio 1917 by Manuel C. Gonzales, A. M. Love, and B. F. Patterson. Gonzales was a native San Antonian who attended a business college in San Antonio and eventually worked for the law firm of Love & Patterson as a legal secretary. Pycior credits Gonzales with persuading Love and Patterson to help Mexican Americans.

The Liga Protectora Mexicana was similar in structure to the mutual-aid societies common in Texas in the early 1920s. Liga members paid one dollar their first year and then five dollars annually afterward. Members received legal advice and, when needed, legal representation. By 1920, the Liga's membership numbered 500, mostly in San Antonio. The cases the Liga took on included labor contracts, land tenancy, and issues concerning law enforcement.[11] Beyond the direct assistance to its members, the Liga also published a weekly column on legal rights in San Antonio's *El Imparcial de Texas*. Opinion pieces centered on a wide range of topics, including public education, laws regarding loans, and land-tenant rights.[12] If Mexican Americans understood their rights and took collective action, then "authorities could be compelled to respect their rights."[13]

Pycior found that the relationship with the Anglo attorneys Love and Patterson was advantageous—it opened a door into the judiciary—but it was also constricting: "This reliance on 'outsiders' kept the membership from organizing for social change in the manner of some of the labor *mutualistas*. The Liga never filed class-action suits or confronted segregation; strikes were considered disruptive. . . . Nevertheless, the Liga did lobby in Austin for some specific reforms."[14]

Among the causes the Liga advocated was a law that would prohibit law enforcement authorities from "aiding or accompanying anyone in acquiring possession . . . of any property, except when the sheriff or other official has a written mandate from the court." Another issue restricted growers from selling tenants' harvest without their consent.[15]

In 1920, the Liga changed its name to the Liga Instructiva Mexicana, Inc., signaling a change in focus: it was now dedicated to preparing Mexicans for U.S. citizenship tests. Manuel Gonzalez quit the Liga and, in 1921, revitalized the legal defense functions of the effort with a new organization called Asociación Jurídica Mexicana "to familiarize *mexicanos* with the origin, goals, substance, and social effect of the laws and customs of the State of Texas . . . and if required [it] will give personal attention to cases."[16] But within the year, that organization had ceased to function.

The Asociación Jurídica Mexicana's effectiveness at combating discrimination was limited, Pycior says, because it lacked funding and "especially, [because of] their precarious position in Texas society. They avoided radical violent protest, preferring to be ignored by the Anglo press and work in relative autonomy. Also, since some of the members were small shopkeepers, class solidarity was often stymied, except in the mutualist labor groups."[17]

In the early 1900s, La Liga Protectora Mexicana printed pamphlets on social service networks, or insurance, and organized protests.[18] Still, Cynthia Orozco concludes that "essential elements for effective organization were missing: there were no statewide Spanish-language newspapers, few paved roads, and few cars. Local defense committees emerged in San Antonio, Houston, and Austin, often led by *mutualistas* in a regional network."[19]

Orozco attributes the emergence of civil rights efforts in the 1920s to returning World War I veterans: "As a class these men developed a political consciousness of U.S. citizenship."[20] One of the organizations that sprang up was the Order Sons of America, which splintered but was nonetheless active in civil rights efforts in South Texas for seven years.[21] Orozco focuses on the League of United Latin American Citizens (LULAC), formed in 1929 in Corpus Christi from a merger of four organizations: the Order Sons of America, the Order Knights of America, the Order Sons of Texas, and the League of Latin American Citizens (LLAC). Orozco says LULAC's name was "a way for México Texanos to assert 100 percent U.S. citizenship and a reminder to Mexican immigrants that they were not eligible to join."[22]

World War I had sparked a new emphasis on civil rights, with returning veterans like José de la Luz Sáenz, who wrote about Mexican Americans in the Great War in his book *Los México-Americanos en la Gran Guerra.*[23] Another World War I civil rights activist was Alonso W. Perales, who went on to law school and became a major figure in civil rights efforts.

Perales also wrote a book, *En Defensa de Mi Raza*.[24] He was a frequent and forceful critic of the discrimination against Mexican Americans.[25]

But Mexican civil rights gained momentum after World War II, when returning Mexican American veterans were determined to challenge the disparities their people faced. In California, returning Mexican American veterans formed the Community Service Organization (CSO), which took on school inequities, police brutality, and voter registration.[26] In 1949, the CSO helped to elect Edward Roybal to the Los Angeles City Council—the first Mexican American L.A. city councilman in sixty-eight years.[27] Roybal ran and won on issues of the wholesale disenfranchisement of his people.

Those so inclined—and who had the educational foundation—used the G.I. Bill to attend college or trade school; some finished law school. In some cases, activists worked through existing organizations, such as LULAC. They also created new organizations, like the American G.I. Forum, founded by a Mexican immigrant physician, Hector P. Garcia. The forum's initial focus was equal treatment for returning Mexican American veterans, but it soon became more politically involved.[28]

To be sure, lawsuits were filed—and sometimes even won. But courtroom challenges were hamstrung too often by juries that included no Mexican Americans. Even in legal victories, plaintiffs learned that in different courtrooms precedents went unrecognized. In hundreds of communities, change occurred case by case, one problem at a time, a gradual redress.

Advances came more quickly in the 1960s, attributable in part to a critical mass of Mexican Americans with greater awareness of the societal strictures that stood in the way of a fuller participation. One of the most dramatic and emblematic events was in the small town of Crystal City, Texas, in 1963 and again in 1970. Crystal, or Cristál in Spanish, was in the early 1960s about 80 percent Mexican American, but the majority held no political office. In 1963, Mexican Americans successfully fielded a slate of five city council candidates, known as "Los Cinco." Political scientist Armando Navarro details the many steps required to politicize Cristál's Mexican American majority. Those steps included exposing corruption among Anglo officeholders, attaining better job prospects and increasing educational opportunities for Mexican Americans, and forming in 1960 the Viva Kennedy Clubs.[29] Another factor was the organization of a chapter of the Political Association of Spanish-speaking Organizations (PASSO), which, in 1963, worked with the International Brotherhood of Teamsters (IBT), or Teamsters Union, to help Mexican Americans pay their $1.75 poll tax. Navarro writes that the effort yielded key results: in Crystal City in 1960, 683 Anglos and 646 Mexican had paid their poll taxes. Two years later, Anglo registration was 538, compared to 795 Mexican Americans registered. And in 1963, Mexicans made up 1,139 of the 1,681 registered voters.[30] When Los Cinco, the Citizens Committee slate, were all elected in April 1963, the "revolt" drew national—and international—attention. The victory was short-lived, for some of the new councilmen suffered retaliation from employers. In the next election cycle, a new PASSO slate lost. Despite its fragile positioning, the 1963 Los Cinco had demonstrated a new energy and possibility to Anglo and Mexican American alike.[31]

Other developments followed: a second taking of Crystal City and the founding of the Raza Unida Party in 1970. And along the way, the social disparities of Mexican Americans became the subject of national news: a television network carried a major story on hunger in San Antonio; a Los Angeles public television station commissioned a series on the growing Chicano movement; and other social issues were laid out for the first time. These developments form the backdrop for the three case studies that this book centers around.

There were major events and activities throughout the Southwest, efforts to desegregate and integrate schools and civil service departments, such as police and fire. MALDEF—the Mexican American Legal Defense and Educational Fund—was incorporated and organized in San Antonio in the late 1960s, with the support and participation of Mexican American attorneys throughout the Southwest. In short, Mexican Americans faced segregation and inequality throughout the region and the Midwest as well. But then as now, the majority of the Mexican American population resided in the Southwest.

One issue that emerged repeatedly in the research for this book was the importance of identity—specifically, how people referred to themselves. At one point, a Ford Foundation executive queried Pete Tijerina, founder of MALDEF, about whether the term "Mexican American" might not antagonize other Spanish-speaking Americans. During the same period, the term "Chicano" suggested a bolder identity. Those who adopted it bristled at the term "Mexican American," which they considered too allied with the establishment, too assimilationist, too conservative.[32]

My goal here is to shed light on three important milestones in Texas's Mexican civil rights advancements. Two of these three case studies, one in Alpine and the other in El Paso, describe the extraordinary steps that were taken to secure equal treatment. The third examines the personalities involved and the compromises required in the creation of a national civil rights organization.

TWO PARTS, THREE CHAPTERS

This book is divided into two parts. The first part deals with civil rights struggles at the local level. The second delves into the creation of a national organization that has fought countless battles, both as collective action lawsuits as well as in defense of individuals.

In the first chapter, the focus is on the Alpine public schools, which were segregated until 1969, and only after the intervention of newly elected Mexican American legislators. That the schools would remain separate until long past 1954, when the U.S. Supreme Court declared that separate schools were inherently unconstitutional, underscores the issue of race for Mexican Americans. Early Mexican American leaders argued that Reconstruction-era state laws, mandating the segregation of African American students, did not apply to Mexican Americans because they were white. Because of that, school authorities bent on maintaining separate facilities for Mexican American children could maintain variously that the different facilities were required for language reasons (it was common for Mexican American children to speak limited English), or, school officials argued, it would be in the best interest of Mexican American children to attend neighborhood schools—in their own segregated neighborhoods. Because Mexican American legal strategy to desegregate schools was based not only on whiteness but also on "a class apart," it was argued that Mexican Americans were "white"—or Caucasian—and so they should therefore enjoy the same privileges and rights as the dominant white, non-Latino population. The landmark *Brown v. Board of Education* decision (1954) offered little relief. Officials could argue that Mexican Americans were not being segregated racially but rather for other reasons—either geographic or because of language. This chapter includes word-for-word transcriptions of interviews that swing back and forth between Spanish and English, conducted with Alpine parents and supporters who sought to force school authorities to provide the best education for Mexican American children. While the transcriptions may be difficult to follow at first, I hope they preserve and convey the flavor of the interviews and underscore how the language issue was front and center of why these parents wished to integrate the schools.

Some critics have ascribed motives for the insistence of some Mexican American leaders to be considered "white" rather than tackling the larger and more important issue: why should any type of racial segregation be tolerated? Alcalá and Rangel put it this way. Before *Brown v. Board of Education* in 1954, separate-but-equal was the law: "[E]arly Chicano attorneys sought acceptance of the mestizo race as white. Chicano cases, therefore, stressed the Fourteenth Amendment's due process and statutory violations, emphasizing segregation in the *absence* of state law, while Black cases were stressing the Fourteenth Amendment equal protection, arguing that segregation in the *presence* of state law was inherently unequal." [33]

There may be many different reasons for that insistence on claiming whiteness. Activists may have chosen that path as a more immediate and pragmatic settlement. Many surely believed that they were more closely "white" than "black." Time and again, the country imposed a black and white binary on race, denying the very existence and presence of Asians, Native Americans, Mexican Americans. In fact, separation papers for Latino World War II military veterans clearly demonstrate this point: some are categorized as "white" and others as "Mexican" and a few as "NA." [34] It wasn't until 1970 that in order to recognize people of Spanish-speaking ethnicities the Census Bureau adopted the category "Hispanic," which was met with varying levels of approval. [35]

There is also an issue of a perceived rivalry between Mexican Americans and African Americans. Some Mexican American advocates felt that African Americans had made more progress than they had, even in instances in which a government agency was charged with helping *all* disadvantaged people. In one example, in testimony before the U.S. Civil Rights Commission, it is noted that the commission itself had concentrated its efforts on African Americans and paid scant attention to Mexican Americans. [36]

The second chapter in part 1 considers the cases of the integration of public safety ranks. In the border town of El Paso, it wasn't until after 1957, and the election of the first Mexican American mayor, Raymond Telles, that there was substantial movement to remove barriers to the hiring of Spanish-surnamed applicants. That story involves the context of Telles's election, the importance of civil service jobs, and how Hispanic people were represented in government ranks at the federal level in the 1960s.

Part 2, chapter 3, sheds light and answers questions about the creation of MALDEF that until now had not been answered. [37] Despite MALDEF's importance and its pivotal role in bringing justice to the larger Mexican American community, there has not yet been a book-length treatment. This book considers MALDEF from its incorporation in 1967 until its move to San Francisco in 1972. It outlines the efforts of Pete Tijerina, a World War II veteran originally from Laredo and transplanted to San Antonio, who took on the monumental task of creating a legal defense group dedicated to righting wrongs against Mexican Americans. It examines the challenges and pressures MALDEF faced outside of the judicial system. This chapter also looks at the role played by the Ford Foundation and its interest in the Mexican American civil rights movement. Finally, it looks at how MALDEF's first board was forced to compromise to survive.

THE REALITY OF HISTORY

At the close of an interview in Alpine in the summer of 2012, one woman stared out her screen door and recalled the Anglo principal of the Centennial School, the exclusively Mexican American school. A monograph about the Centennial School, published in 1982, had characterized the principal as a fair and supportive administrator. But this woman had seen another side of him—a side that kept Mexican American children in a subservient position. The woman had meant to bring that point up to the monograph's writer, she said, but he died before she could. She regretted that.

So it is that this book represents my effort to provide as full and honest a portrayal of the events and individuals involved that I can. I make no effort to place the World War II generation on a higher moral ground than that which we stand on today.[38] I have neither sought out, nor avoided, evidence of disagreements, controversies, or shortcomings. I have, to the best of my ability, sought to tell the history as I have found it and to interpret it in a way that brings about a better understanding of that history.

Lastly, I wrote this book with the intention of making it accessible to a general audience while still providing fresh interpretations and information to those academics who are familiar with these topics. In this way, I aspire to the ideals of the Latino scholars who precede me, people like Ernesto Galarza, who wanted the people to be able to see themselves in those writings, so that his writing would be useful for the people about whom he wrote.[39]

PART 1

Claiming Rights on a Local Level

ONE

Integration *a* Mordidas *in Alpine Schools*

The caravan of cars, six or seven of them, made their way south-east on Highway 90 from Alpine at about noon one bright August day in 1969. Some of the travelers met at Our Lady of Peace, the small Catholic church on the Mexican side of town. Others were picked up at their homes. One car was driven by Pete Gallego Sr., a school board member who had borrowed his sister's new Cadillac for the occasion. Another car was driven by another school board member, Johnny Sotelo, traveling with his brother, Frank, as well as Virginia Dominguez and her friend Celia Gomez Ramirez. Virginia Dominguez, who was forty-one at the time, recalled later that to pass the time — radio reception was spotty for long stretches — Johnny Sotelo and his brother urged her to sing. She complied, full throated, belting out the *rancheras* preferred by Mexican Americans of her generation. "Cielito Lindo" was a favorite. At the midway point, two hundred miles south of Alpine, the caravan stopped at the edge of Amistad Lake in Del Rio for a lunch of bologna and cheese sandwiches, chips, and soft drinks. Dominguez made sure to bring the chili peppers she relished with every meal, eating them raw, "*a mordidas*," biting off a bit with her food.[1] After that respite, they drove the next 230 miles east and then north to Austin.

Elidia Leyva, then thirty-five, and Mary Pallanez, then thirty-one, both department store clerks, traveled in the car driven by Pete Gallego. Pallanez recalled later that the mood was light, with laughter and chitchat. These men and women had known one another all their lives, growing up in the small community of Alpine. But their chumminess belied the serious objective of the twenty-seven men and women, and two teenage boys, who were en route to the state capital to meet with the Texas education commissioner, to ask him to intercede, to force the desegregation of public schools in their West Texas town. They had tried just about everything else. But since it was built in 1936 to commemorate the 100th anniversary of Texas independence, Centennial School stood on the south side of the tracks in the middle of the barrio, educating only the Mexican American children from first to eighth grade, while Central, the school north of the tracks, was the Anglo school. Only a very few intrepid Mexican American students willing to face ostracism from their own, as well as possible rejection from Anglo classmates, attended the Anglo school. Alpine High School, the only high school in town, was integrated, but many Mexican Americans dropped out before they got there.

"It was a fun trip," Leyva recalled more than forty years after the caravan journey to Austin.

> *Pero a lo que ibamos, pues* [But because of what we were going for, well] it was no fun, *porque ibamos a pelear—no a pelear—pero a lo que oiréan la razón por que ibamos allí* [because we were going to fight, no—not to fight—but so that they would hear the reason that we were going there]. And it didn't take long, *pero lo poquito que hablaron alli,* [but the little that was said there] it helped. That's what started the whole thing, that's what started the whole thing.

That "whole thing" was, in 1969, the integration of Alpine public schools.

HISTORY OF CENTENNIAL

Alpine sits in a valley, the foothills of the Davis Mountains encircling it. This is the high desert in Texas, 4,476 feet above sea level. It is so dry that, unlike most parts of Texas, "the heat is never oppressive in the summer . . . and there are no mosquitos and absolutely no malaria," boosters wrote in the early 1900s. In fact, it is so arid that carcasses "of dead animals do not decompose in the usual way but dry up on the plains."[2] City leaders likened Alpine's temperate climate to "that of Southern France."[3] It was a favorable location in another way as well. Early residents could rely on a shallow water table, only twenty to forty feet deep, to dig their wells.[4] The water table was a key reason for Alpine's attraction. In this western part of the state, fifteen inches of precipitation in one year is considered almost tropical; the next year rainfall may be less than two inches.

It was the construction of the Southern Pacific main line, cutting east to west through Brewster County, and completed in the 1880s, that brought Mexican settlers to this land:

> During the late winter and early spring of 1882, as the construction crews were building the railroad through the mountains from Paisan Pass eastward toward what is now the Alpine valley, families of the Mexican-American workers of the construction crews moved into the valley and pitched their tents along what is now Alpine Creek in an effort to keep in touch with their men folks who were working on the railroad. Thus these Mexican-American families were to become the first permanent settlers of what was to become Alpine, Texas.[5]

The 1890 census showed there were more than twice as many Mexican Americans as Anglos in Alpine: 605 to 275 Anglos.[6] Apparently, the Mexicans were largely the laborer class, whereas the Anglos were the supervisors and owners of small businesses, such as the Holland Hotel and Forchheimer's Department Store, that would come later.[7] But over time, there were also Mexican-owned businesses, grocery stores (one owned by Clemente J. Uranga), and a few restaurants. One of the earliest Mexican American settlers was a woman named María Moreno, who was a *curandera*, or faith healer.[8]

Although this West Texas town's name evokes images of snow and skiing, Alpine is none of that. Instead, the native plants here are hardy— they can get by on annual rainfall of less than two inches. The predominant plants here include sotol, lechuguilla, and Candelilla. Before it was called Alpine, the town was known as Murphyville, taken from Thomas O. Murphy, who sold the railroad water rights for its steam engines.[9] One legend attributes the name "Alpine" to a group of men waiting for the mail to be "put up" at the post office. One flipped open a postal guide, which listed the names of the cities and towns throughout the country. It fell open to Alpine, Alabama. He then thumbed through the Texas section of the guide, which listed all the state's cities and towns, and finding no Alpine, Texas, he mused that Alpine might be a good new name.[10] After all, if Alabama could have an Alpine, why not Texas? In 1888, ninety residents registered their vote, and Murphyville became Alpine.[11]

A 1909 booklet, which apparently sought to lure businesses to Alpine by outlining the city's strengths, features a photo of Alpine High School, a stately two-story building, which had been recently completed for a price tag of $35,000.[12] There is no mention about whether Mexican Americans were admitted into that school, but a newspaper story in 1901 announced the building of a new school, known simply as "the Mexican School." In 1917, the Mexican School was given a proper name, Francisco E. Madero Ward School, a public school named for the Mexican president whom many historians generally credit with sparking the Mexican Revolution in 1911.[13] The school was also known as "La Escuela de Don Clemente," in tribute to the previously mentioned Clemente J. Uranga, who owned a small grocery store in Alpine, and who, according to his son, Charlie V. Uranga, was instrumental in its building, because there had been no such facilities for Mexican Americans.[14] A Catholic school, the School of the Sacred Heart, was established on October 22, 1919, by the Catholic nuns of the order Servants of the Sacred Heart and of the Poor.[15] It was referred to as the "the Sister School," or la Escuela de las Madres (the School of the Nuns).[16] But there was apparently a third school, a Methodist school in the 1920s, begun by the Mexican Methodist pastor and his wife, Esau Perez and Febronia Florian Muñoz, who were assigned to Alpine. Evidence is a photograph of a group of children, captioned 1926.[17] There was a separate school for black children, the Morgan School, named for Morgan Gordon, an African American landowner who sold the Black Methodist Episcopal Convention of Texas a plot for ten dollars for that purpose.[18] In 1936, the public school for Mexican American children was built and named the Centennial School in honor of the state of Texas's centenary anniversary.

The fact that there were three different schools—one for Anglos, a second for Mexican Americans, and a third for black children—was partly due to a provision in the post–Civil War state constitution, adopted in 1876, which mandated separate schools for white and colored children.[19] The segregation of Mexican American children was not explicitly mandated; it was instead de facto—by habit and custom. After the 1954 *Brown v. Board of Education* Supreme Court decision outlawed segregated schools, the African American children were enrolled in the Mexican American school, Centennial. The *Alpine Avalanche* carried a front-page story, "Racial Segregation in Alpine's Public Schools Abolished," and said that the Alpine Board of Trustees voted to desegregate the schools "after considerable discussion of the problem." Seven "Negro" children would be integrated into various grade sections.[20] One account said that the African American children "chose to enroll at Centennial," since they lived in south Alpine, which was mostly Mexican American, and that the African

American children "were familiar with Hispanics and their culture."[21] But it is more likely, given the racial climate, that the African American children would have been unwelcome at the Anglo school, as were the Mexican American children.

The Mexican American men and women who were parents of the Centennial School students in 1969 were mostly native to Alpine, or they were born in nearby towns and then relocated to Alpine. In interviews with them, they slipped unselfconsciously between Spanish and English—often more than once in a sentence.[22] It is a practice that linguists call "code-switching." It's also the manner of speaking that many Latino novelists and playwrights try to capture, as it signifies a straddling of cultures, a loyalty to the language of one's forebears but a recognition that English is, after all, the language of business and education in the United States.

In these parts, among Mexican Americans who are in their fifties and older, the use of language marks the difference between their English-speaking public life and the Spanish-speaking or bilingual private hearth. It is also, not coincidentally, a good measure of the level of acculturation among Latinos.

In interviews here, some Mexican Americans use the word *Americanos* to refer to Anglos. But the use of *Americanos* by Mexican Americans—who are also Americans, of course—also suggests a lingering tension with the past. This land was once part of Mexico. After the Mexican-American War, it became part of the United States, and the people here of Mexican descent faced a world of diminished status; they were, "a conquered population."[23] Researchers have long identified this problem, noting that the indigenous population of the Southwest was subjugated and colonized by the Spaniards; and then it was recolonized by Anglo Americans. During hearings before the U.S. Civil Rights Commission in 1968, Jack P. Forbes, a historian and anthropologist who was also a leader in Native American Studies, addressed that past:

> One must of course get past the romance and mythology of the supposed westward movement of the pioneers and look at the Anglo-American conquest of the Southwest as we might look at the German march eastward against the Poles or as we might look at the Franco-Norman conquest of England, in other words, in a purely detached and objective manner. . . . [Were that detachment accomplished, we] would see the U.S. conquest of the Southwest as a very real case of aggres-

sion and imperialism, that it involved not only the military phase of immediate conquest, but the subsequent establishment of a colonial society.[24]

There were, at various times, efforts to "Americanize" Mexican Americans, as well as other ethnic groups, like German Americans.[25] Guadalupe San Miguel writes that pre–World War I, the Americanization movement was benign, seeking to help immigrants adjust to their new country. But after World War I, the objective changed: rather than immigrants assimilating into U.S. culture, they were expected to cut ties to their culture and language to be considered loyal Americans. In Texas, that new approach took the form of legislation. In 1918, a bill was passed that would make English the exclusive language of public schools, not only for teachers and students, but for administrators, school board members, and all other public school staff.[26] Teaching in any language other than English was criminalized, a misdemeanor punishable by a fine of between twenty five and one hundred dollars, as well as "revocation of state teacher certificate, automatic dismissal . . . if a word of non-English instruction was uttered."[27] That law stayed on the books, modified only slightly, until a Bilingual Education Act was passed in 1973.

Those were the times that these Mexican American proponents of school integration in Alpine had grown up in, an atmosphere hostile to their language and, by extension, to their culture. When they started first grade, they spoke only Spanish, as it was the language of the home. As they advanced, they were expected to speak only English at school. Those who spoke to their friends in Spanish on school grounds were punished.

Language, then, is central to the Alpine integration story.

PRETTY ENGLISH

Virginia Dominguez, for instance, noticed that many of the Mexican American children in Alpine spoke only broken English. She grew up in Alpine, but after she married and started her own family, her husband's job, as a carpenter for oil companies, took her and her family to small West Texas towns with names like Crane, Seminole, and Kermit, to the city of Midland, and to neighboring Roswell, New Mexico. "*Estos jugaban con americanitos y ellos hablaban muy bonito el ingles* [These (her children) played with the American children and they spoke English very nicely]," Dominguez said.[28]

FIGURE 1.1. *Virginia and Isidoro S. Dominguez, 1975.*
Courtesy of the Voces Oral History Project.

In Alpine, though, the Mexican American children spoke poor English, because, Dominguez concluded, they were not interacting with the
English-speaking Anglo children. *"Me gustó la idea* [I liked the idea],"
Dominguez said, referring to integrating the schools. Dominguez had
gone only as far as the fifth grade herself. In her day, Dominguez said,
many parents, including her own, didn't stress an education. Parents even
discouraged their daughters from attending school:

"No, pa' que me ayudes a lavar." Y yo, pues contenta, encantada de la
vida, nos quedábamos [en casa] a no tener que ir a la escuela.

["No, so you'll help me with the laundry." And I, well, was happy,
thrilled, to stay home and not have to go to school.]

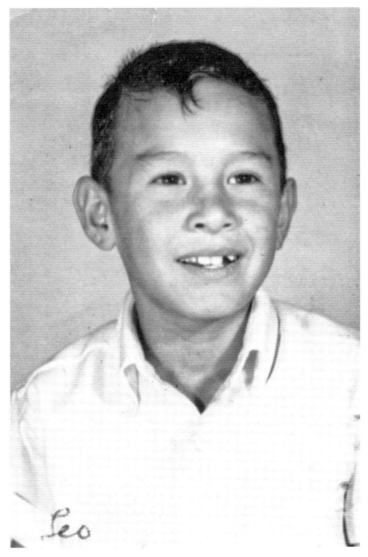

Figure 1.2. *Leo Dominguez, ca. 1963. Courtesy of the Voces Oral History Project.*

When Dominguez and her family moved back to Alpine, her young son, Leo, enrolled in Centennial. But his smooth, unaccented English, from years in integrated schools in other small towns, marked him. He was conspicuous among the other Mexican American youngsters, whose English was labored and heavily accented. Leo found himself chased and beaten by the other Mexican American boys: he was an outsider, his good English a clear giveaway. Leo would come home for lunch and often resisted returning to school in the afternoon, dreading the bullies—they were bigger and knew how to fight. By the fifth grade, Leo Dominguez had had enough; he transferred to Central, the Anglo school. There the teachers treated him well. He had trouble with some of the boys—not all, but some. But the Anglo boys weren't as good fighters as the Mexican American boys, and Leo could handle himself against them.[29]

Violeta Dominguez understood the deeper problem. It was more than little boys tormenting the new kid in town. The boys couldn't articulate it and were perhaps unaware of their resentment against a system that deemed Spanish the inferior language, that restricted Mexican Americans to the Centennial School and the poorer neighborhoods south of the tracks. The boys had no way of fighting the system; whom would they attack? But what they could do was beat up on the innocent Leo. His good English symbolized the dual system. Dominguez believed that the hostility could be avoided if all children attended the same school: speaking good English should not be a stigma.

Not that the separate schools seemed like such a problem for all in the Mexican American community. Angelita Ramirez Valenzuela, for instance, took her children to the Catholic school, La Escuela de las Madres, where the nuns required tuition only in the amount of "whatever [one] could afford," Valenzuela said. She and her husband, Francisco, paid about $1.50 a month for their children to attend the school. Francisco Valenzuela had a good job, a steady job, working for the local electrical company, so they could afford it. And the Catholic school offered a good, strict education:

> *No había allí con "ahora no vine," y "mañana a ver." Y mi* husband, *también [estaba de acuerdo]. So aprendieron mucho aquí con las madres— buenas para ensenar. Y la disciplina y todo, muy bien.*

> [And there was none of the "I didn't go today" and "maybe tomorrow." And my husband [was] also [in agreement]. So [my children] learned

a lot with the nuns—[they were] good at teaching. And the discipline, everything—very good.]

Although Valenzuela was indifferent to integrating the school, she also didn't object to it.

> *Pero habia mucha gente que* [But there were many people] they really cared, *querían que sus hijos se juntaran con los otros* [They wanted their children to associate with the others (Anglos)] *Pero, como le digo* [But like I tell you], I didn't care much at the time because my children were going to Catholic school, they were getting a good education. I guess I was used to *[que] ellos estuvieran alla al otro lado del park* [that the Anglos were over there on the other side of the park]. I guess I was used to it. I haven't given it too much thought. But like I say, most people did care. It didn't matter too much for me at that time. *Ya despues, pues, sí, si así es la ley, debe de estar así la escuela. ¿Por que nó?* [Later, well, yes, if that's the law, the school should be that way (integrated). Why not?][30]

Mary Pallanez, sitting in Elidia Leyva's living room one sunny August afternoon in 2012, recalled those years before the integration as pleasant. Pallanez didn't have children of her own; she had gone on the 1969 caravan trip to Austin because she had nieces and she wanted integrated schools for them. And yet, when she had been a student a few years before the caravan, she didn't see anything so bad about the separate schools.

"We didn't know any better. We didn't question it. We had the railroad track, that's what divided us," Pallanez said. "We grew up thinking it was the right thing."[31]

But Leyva shook her head slowly and firmly.

"I don't feel that way, Mary. *Porque pa' mi, todo el tiempo . . . Entonces estaba los traques. Y todo la gente mexicana vivían aquí y los americanos vivían de allá. Los americanos no pasaban pa'ca para este lado.*" [Because for me, all the time . . . At that time there were (train) tracks. And all the Mexican people lived here and the Americans lived over there. The Americans didn't come to this side.][32]

There were teachers at Centennial who earned the respect and affection of their students. One was Mrs. Berta Clark Lassiter, who served as principal of Madero Ward until it was closed. After that, Lassiter taught at Centennial and she was one of the few Anglos in Alpine with whom

FIGURE 1.3. *The Bertas, May 1955. Standing, left to right: Berta Portillo and Berta Gallego; seated, left to right: Berta Ramos, Berta Natera Fierro, Mrs. Berta Lassiter, Berta Valadez, and Berta Cadena. Seated on Mrs. Lassiter's lap is Berta Uranga, and on Mrs. Valdez's lap is Berta Alicia De La O. Courtesy of the Archives of the Big Bend, Bryan Wildenthal Memorial Library, Sul Ross State University.*

Mexican American children interacted on a daily basis; she treated her students and their families with respect. Lassiter became a major figure for her students, so much so that many former students named their own daughters for her. One photograph of Lassiter features her sitting with four Mexican American women with their four daughters, all girls whom the women had named Berta, in honor of their beloved teacher.[33]

But there were other teachers who were remembered for their harshness, some who paddled students for speaking Spanish on school grounds. The children's own parents wouldn't advocate for their children. If a child was punished at school, and told her parents, they would question what she had done wrong, Pallanez and Leyva agreed.

Leyva was an athlete all through school—at Centennial and later at Alpine High School. There is one incident that burned in her heart many

FIGURE 1.4. *Centennial Girls Volleyball. Top row, left to right: Velma Gallegos, Enedina Lujan, Elidia Gallego [Leyva], and Lorena Aguilar; bottom row, left to right: Alicia Molinari, Dora Lujan, and Fabiola Hernandez, 1950. Courtesy of the Archives of the Big Bend, Bryan Wildenthal Memorial Library, Sul Ross State University.*

years later; she regretted that she hadn't spoken up for herself. Leyva's athleticism was undeniable: she excelled in volleyball and basketball; many of the other Mexican American girls and boys were also competitive. "*No nos ganaban nadie* [No one could beat us]," she said. At an annual assembly at Alpine High School, the athletes were usually recognized, presented with their trophies or jackets in front of the entire school. But this one year, when Leyva must have been a junior, the school principal dealt the Mexican American girls a humiliating blow.

> *Y entonces cuando iban a tener ese* assembly. *Nos llamaron todas las mejicanas del* team—*todas las mejicanas del* team—*y tenían todas las chaquetas allí en la oficina, y nos dijeron que nó nos iban a dar las* awards *en el* assembly *porque nos habíamos portado muy mal, que* we didn't deserve to be presented those awards in the assembly and that's why we were given those awards there. *Y que sí no entendíamos—ya estabamos en* high school—*que sí no entiendiamos ingles, tenían un* Spanish teacher *allí, que era americano pero hablaba español muy bien*; he was a Spanish teacher, *el Slover. Que si no entendíamos muy bien, él nos iba a interpretar.*
>
> Up to this day, *digo yo, porque no le agarré yo la chaqueta y le dije,* "Stick it where the sun doesn't shine"?[34]

[And then they were going to have this assembly. They called all the Mexican girls from the team—all the Mexican girls from the team—and they had the jackets there in the office, and they told us that they were not going to give us the awards in the assembly because we had behaved very badly, that we didn't deserve to be presented those awards in the assembly and that's why we were given those awards there. And that if we didn't understand—we were already in high school—that if we didn't understand English, they had a Spanish teacher there, *el* Slover. That if we didn't understand very well, he would translate. Up to this day, I tell myself, Why didn't I take that jacket and tell him, "Stick it where the sun doesn't shine"?]

The insult was triple. The girls were being told they had misbehaved, without being told what their offense was, and for that reason they were undeserving; that they didn't deserve the public recognition usually bestowed upon the school's athletes; and perhaps most telling, that even as high school students they may not have mastered English enough to understand what was being said. For Leyva, it was an unmistakable attack on the girls' ethnicity: a clear reminder that they were different and that no matter their accomplishments, they would not be respected.

Years later, it was Leyva's inaction in the face of the affront that caused her so much remorse. She and her friends had been passive; they should have challenged the principal. But, she adds, these teenaged girls were powerless, and with no support.

> *Nos dejábamos que nos dijeran cosas que esto y este otro, porque no teníamos nadie que nos backiara, que nos protejieran, que hablara por nosotros ... ellos [school officials] mandaban, ellos mandaban, todo mandaban. ... It was bad, it was very bad.*

> [We let them tell us things, this and that, because we didn't have anyone who would back us up, who would protect us, who would speak for us. They (school officials) were in charge, they were in charge, they were in charge of everything. It was bad; it was very bad.][35]

A few years later, when Leyva was old enough, and had her own two sons in school, there was no question whether she would take a stand. It may have taken her twenty years, but she wouldn't let the schools get away with telling the next generation of Mexican American children that they didn't measure up.

SEGREGATED SCHOOLS IN TEXAS

Public schools in Texas had long been a battleground for Mexican American civil right advocates. Education was the cornerstone of success; without it, there was little chance for better jobs, decent wages, good housing, free time for civic engagement. Education could lead indirectly to political representation, or at least to elected officials who would take the needs of Mexican Americans seriously. But Mexican Americans in Texas lagged woefully behind all other groups. In 1960, they had an average of only 6.1 years of schooling, an improvement, no doubt, from the 3.6 years in 1950, but still far below the 10.8 years for whites, and 8.1 years for nonwhites.[36] In 1970, George I. Sanchez would testify to the U.S. Commission on Civil Rights that Spanish-surnamed people in Texas over the age of seventeen had 4.7 years of school, compared to 8.1 years for Afri-

FIGURE 1.5. *Centennial Students. Courtesy of the Archives of the Big Bend, Bryan Wildenthal Memorial Library, Sul Ross State University.*

can Americans and 8.1 for the overall population.[37] The number of years of schooling for the Mexican American population of California, New Mexico, Arizona, and Colorado was also lower than for whites and non-whites—but Texas had the unfortunate distinction of the fewest years of schooling for Mexican Americans. Many Texas school districts were segregated, despite court decisions that had outlawed it.

The first case brought against a segregated public school district was *Méndez v. Westminster School District*, filed in California.[38] It came about in September 1943, when Soledad Vidauri took her two daughters and her brother's three children to enroll in school at Westminster Main School. The school officials told Vidauri they would take the two Vidauri girls because they were light skinned and looked "white." But the three other children, her niece and nephews, were darker and were directed to the Mexican school close by. A furious Vidauri refused; her brother and sister-in-law, Gonzalo and Felicitas Méndez, were equally outraged. They and other parents sued four school districts, charging that the plaintiffs and five thousand other Latino students had been segregated into "Mexican schools."[39] A federal court in February 1946 agreed, ruling that the segregated schools violated the equal protection clause of the Fourteenth Amendment, a ruling upheld by the U.S. Court of Appeals for the Ninth Circuit the following year.

Civil rights activists in Texas took note of the California civil rights case and sought to apply the ruling to their own state.[40] The American G.I. Forum and the League of United Latin American Citizens (LULAC) stood at the forefront of Texas efforts; among their advisers was University of Texas professor George I. Sanchez, who sometimes spearheaded fund-raising efforts, including finding foundation grants to pay for litigation. The suits were brought by a small cadre of attorneys who had already been involved in other Mexican American civil rights cases. They included Gus Garcia, Chris Aldrete, James DeAnda, and Carlos Cadena.

But if the Westminster case appeared to signal an opening for Texas Mexican American civil rights proponents, they were a step behind seg-regationist Texas officials. The week before the Ninth Circuit Court of Appeals issued its decision on the Westminster case, then Texas attor-ney general Price Daniel issued an opinion on the segregation of Mexi-can American children. Schools could not separate students "solely on race. . . . But based solely on language deficiencies and other individual needs and aptitudes demonstrated by examination or properly conducted tests, a school district may maintain separate classes in separate build-ings if necessary, for any pupils with such deficiencies, needs or aptitudes through the first three grades." [41]

The wording of Daniel's opinion offered a loophole: segregation based on a lack of English-speaking skills "*or other individual needs and aptitudes demonstrated by examination or properly conducted tests*" was allowed for grades 1–3. In response, the Texas State Board of Education passed a resolution in May 1950 saying segregation of "Latin American" children violated the law, but segregation of those children based on cri-teria other than race was allowed. Texas Education Commissioner J. W. Edgar, the state's top education official, wrote to the state's school super-intendents, county superintendents, and presidents of boards of trustees, notifying them of the new policy and outlining procedures for occasions when segregation was alleged. The letter to the state's school authorities is carefully worded: segregation of "Latin-American" children from "Anglo-American" children is "contrary to law."

> We believe that it is highly desirable for local boards of trustees to be given every opportunity to administer the local school program in accordance with provisions of the statutes. Consistent with this desire

to promote strong local administration of the school program and in order that local authorities may discharge their legal responsibility the following procedure has been adopted to handle cases where it is alleged there exists the practice of segregating Latin-American children from Anglo-American children in the school program.

Those steps, however, favored the schools rather than the complainants:

1. Complaints made to the Commissioner of Education "without evidence of previous action of the local board of trustees . . . will be referred to the local school authorities of the school district involved in order that appropriate action may be taken."
2. If those local authorities found evidence of discrimination, they were required to "make the necessary adjustment in their administrative policy to eliminate this practice."
3. In cases where the complainant is unsatisfied by the local decision, they may appeal to the Commissioner of Education.
4. If the Commissioner of Education finds evidence that the local authorities have violated segregation statutes or "invaded the constitutional rights of children of Latin-American descent, he will take such action as will be appropriate and consistent with the advice and counsel of the Attorney General."[42]

A complaint of discrimination, therefore, would be required to wend its way through three different authorities: first the local school board, then the education commissioner, and finally the attorney general. At a time when there were few Mexican Americans at any level of governmental authority, the likelihood of prevailing through such a chain of authority was obviously remote. That was clear to Mexican Americans. In 1952, the G.I. Forum called on the TEA to reconsider, likening the procedure for challenging discrimination against Mexican American students to that of "asking a jury to reconsider the case of a man it has already found guilty."[43]

The American G.I. Forum and LULAC kept up their pressure—shooting off complaints to the Texas State Board of Education. Responding to one of the complaints from the G.I. Forum in 1952, the superintendent of one small school district twenty-seven miles east of Corpus Christi admitted to segregating the first two years, but argued that it had been in the best interest of the students. Banquete superintendent G. M. Blackman acknowledged that he was responding to a complaint G.I. Forum founder and president Hector P. Garcia had sent to the state board of education. Blackman verified that the first two years of elementary school were segregated "for the advantage and benefit of the American children of Mexican origin in order that they may learn the English language and get acquainted with school habits. It would be unfair for them to place them with children who have gone beyond this obstacle and mastered the difficulties."

But, Blackman said, there was no difference between the quality of instructors, books, water fountains, bathrooms, equipment, school supplies. They use the playgrounds and "sit at the same table with the other children. Furthermore, during the past year we fed forty-one American children of Mexican origin free per day. They enjoy the same privileges and are not abused in any way." Blackman said if his assurances did not satisfy Garcia, Garcia was welcome to visit the school and "make the findings yourself."[44]

Another case was in the Alief school district, seventeen miles west of Houston. In 1950, Alief superintendent F. M. Glaze sought the Texas Education Agency's approval of creating a "no-grade classroom for non-English-speaking children, providing that it will not conflict with non-segregation laws." As background, Glaze said, the Alief schools had a perennial and "serious problem" with its first graders.

"Fifty per cent or more of our beginners are Latin-Americans who do not speak English when they enter school," Glaze wrote. "The teacher has to spend the major portion of her time with this group, which leaves less time for the Anglo-American children." The solution had been to group children according to "learning capacity" and "rate of progress."

"As a result, by the end of their first year, the major portion of the Mexican children have not learned enough English to merit promotion. Several Anglo-American children, due to a lack of adequate attention, fail to make normal progress also. Dicipline [sic] problems arise which might not otherwise exist," Glaze said.[45]

The Texas commissioner of education essentially gave the Alief superintendent free rein to act as he chose: "[W]e act on these matters only when appealed to us from a decision of the local board of education. It will be impossible for us, therefore, until it is actually in operation and an appeal has reached us on that basis, to take action."[46]

The G.I. Forum characterized the commissioner's actions in various school segregation complaints as "dilatory tactics." In its newsletter, the forum told members that the Texas Education Agency could not be counted on for intervention.

> After experiencing the dilatory tactics followed by Edgar on some ten appeals carried to him during the past four or five years, it has been determined that it will be far less costly and more effective to go straight into Federal Court on cases of this type rather than lay them before the Commissioner. An example of the dilatory tactics followed by Edgar is the Mathis School Segregation Case on which he granted a hearing for May 11 only recently. The case was *initially* called to his attention almost two years ago.[47]

The forum noted that Edgar's predecessor, L. A. Woods, who withdrew accreditation of schools "*after* notice to them but without even insisting on a local hearing much less a hearing before him in Austin."

> An example of this was the Del Rio case which was called to Woods' attention in the fall of 1948. Woods immediately sent his first assistant to Del Rio who after investigation advised the Del Rio authorities that they were practicing segregation.
>   Woods shortly thereafter advised them that if they did not rectify the condition, he would withdraw their accreditation. When they refused to comply, he proceeded to withdraw their accreditation without any further *blah, blah, blah and more blah, blah, blah*, about hearings.[48]

The newsletter doesn't mention that the victory in Del Rio was fleeting. Superintendent Woods suffered the consequences of pulling the Del Rio schools' accreditation. Shortly afterward, the Texas Legislature abolished Woods's position, that of the Texas State Superintendent of Schools, and created a new position, Texas State Commissioner of Education, an appointed position. It was a blatant and effective move to control the TEA. The first appointee was the previously mentioned J. W. Edgar.[49] Alcalá and Rangel write that the new law, eliminating Woods's position, was heralded as an "emergency measure," effective July 7, 1949. When Del Rio school officials appealed Superintendent Woods's earlier decision to the new commissioner, J. W. Edgar, Edgar sided with the school district and reversed Woods's decision.[50]

The incident underscored a continuing obstacle: successes were often

temporary when segregationists found ways to overturn them. State officials committed to maintaining the inequality had recognized that as
long as Mexican Americans were politically impotent, they were unable
to change the school system, either through litigation or administratively.

There had been courtroom wins in the state that had appeared to
usher in progress. But even then, segregationists had found ways to cir-
cumvent the law. For instance, in 1948, LULAC sued the Bastrop Independent School District (Bastrop ISD) and three other districts, alleging that
Mexican American children were being segregated despite there being no
state law mandating segregation and in violation of the attorney general's
opinion. *Delgado v. Bastrop*[51] alleged that the Mexican American schools
had inferior instruction, services, and facilities. Judge Ben H. Rice of the
United States District Court, Western District of Texas, ruled in favor of
the plaintiffs and ordered that the segregation be discontinued by September 1949. The only exceptions to the rule were that separate classes, on
the same campus, would be allowed in first grade for children who spoke
little or no English, "as identified by scientific and standardized tests."[52]
San Miguel writes that attorney Gus Garcia sought to pin down Daniel,
asking for details about what circumstances were required before segregation would be allowed. Daniel affirmed that it would only be when test-
ing demonstrated it was necessary. But, San Miguel notes: "[T]he legal
opinion on segregation was ineffective for no mechanism to secure com-
pliance was established nor guidelines for implementing these steps provided to local school officials."[53]

Even after the 1948 Westminster case, *Delgado v. Bastrop* in 1949, and
Brown v. Board of Education in 1954, many Mexican American children
remained in segregated schools, as authorities insisted that the language
barrier was such that the children would be unable to understand their
lessons—and that the Anglo children would be held back. One lawsuit
was filed in 1955 against the Carrizo Springs schools by attorney Chris
Aldrete. In response, the following year a Texas Education Agency official investigated the Carrizo Springs complaint and verified that Mexican
American students were kept apart from Anglo students. But the official was sympathetic to the schools' viewpoint: "The first three grades are
definitely separated on a racial or language basis as a result of a long-time
study made under the supervision of Miss Maurine Gardner, who is the
principal of the elementary school. There is no question that this segregation is being done as an honest attempt to give particularly the Latin
American children a better foundation and beginning for their educational career," wrote the official.[54]

The fourth grade was housed in the same building, with no segregation. There were two classrooms for the Mexican American children in grades 5–8 "who for one reason or another are unable to keep up with the section or grade to which they are regularly assigned." When the children were deemed ready to rejoin their classmates, they were allowed to do so. In the senior high school, there was no discrimination, the official said.

The TEA staffer did not include in his report how the early segregation may have affected the Mexican American schoolchildren later. The 1954 Carrizo Springs High School Yearbook included forty-nine freshmen, and only fifteen, or 31 percent, were Spanish surnamed. Three years later, in 1957, when these freshmen would have been seniors, only two Mexican Americans were left in a class of twenty-seven, or 7 percent, a drop of 24 percentage points. The Carrizo Springs school administration had no Spanish-surnamed officials. Nor were there any on the eight-person board of trustees; none among the three principals, none among the thirty-four-teacher faculty.[55]

But while many of the administrators and policy makers at the local and state levels rejected integration, civil rights activists sought to use their alliances with the Mexican government as leverage. The Good Neighbor Commission, established in 1943 to mollify the Mexican government's fury at ill treatment of Mexicans and Mexican Americans, also noticed how schools were barometers of how Mexicans and Mexican Americans were treated.[56] The Mexican government was threatening to drop two Texas counties from the bracero program, a guest worker program that permitted U.S. employers to hire Mexican laborers. The Mexican government played the role of gatekeeper: if it determined that Mexicans faced discrimination in a county, it could pull braceros from that county. The Mexican consul had complained that there was a disparity in the quality of public school facilities and teachers in two South Texas counties. "Unless equal facilities in class room space, sanitation, general appearances, and teachers's [sic] training are given these pupils, they will continue . . . under the impression that they are penalized for being 'Mexicans.'"[57] The Good Neighbor Commission also criticized the curriculum and textbooks, saying that a "false, chauvinistic treatment of history . . . has perpetuated prejudice and ignorance of our international relations and it has tortured generations of Texas-born school children who would like to be proud of both their Mexican and Texas origin and are not allowed to be proud of either."[58]

That economic threat of losing braceros—a loss to the agricultural industry—appeared to put Texas Education Commissioner Edgar on alert. Edgar received a letter from the Texas Employment Commission about the same issue, saying that the Mexican Embassy in Washington had warned about problems in Robstown and Banquete. "If at the beginning of this next school year, this alleged discrimination continues, the counties will definitely be placed on the ineligible list—which may lead to cancellation of [labor] contracts in existence at that time," the TEC official wrote.[59] Banquete and Robstown are within a half hour's drive from Corpus Christi. Edgar promptly wrote to school superintendent G. M. Blackman in Banquete and B. C. Banks in Robstown: "I am sure you will want to review your policy in this matter and perhaps advise me, or, if you prefer, write directly to Mr. LeBlanc in regard to the practices which exist in the Banquete [and Robstown] schools."[60]

Edgar's archives reveal only a few clues as to the prevailing sentiment among non-Mexican Americans regarding school desegregation. One May 1955 letter writer complained about the G.I. Forum and about the "howling" from "Latin Americans."

> I lived in Kingsville for just a few weeks and it was all we could take.
> Mathis is almost as bad . . . [I]t isn't the Latin-American who should
> be howling but the white citizens. In one town the Mexican kids were
> so crawling with lice that they had to be bathed by the teachers every
> few mornings. If our children had been forced into classes with some
> of these filthy kids, who chattered in Spanish all day long, it wouldn't
> be long before our children would be speaking Spanish instead of
> English. I don't want my little 1st grade daughter sitting next to a Mexi-
> can child whose head was crawling with lice and who hadn't had a bath
> for a month and neither would you, and it's just about time we pinned
> this G.I. Forum down and laid our cards on the table.[61]

Edgar's response to the letter writer was noncommittal; he merely thanked her for sharing her perspective.[62]

THE SHOWDOWN

Social structures were shifting by the mid-1960s; segregation of public facilities was no longer tenable. The 1964 federal Civil Rights Act outlawed discrimination on the basis of race, color, religion, gender, or national origin. But as far as school desegregation, it was the provision in Title VI of the Civil Rights Act that offered a possible tool: it called for desegregating "any program or activity receiving Federal financial assistance." Schools, dependent on federal funding, were now made accountable to federal laws.

On a parallel track, the Mexican American, or Chicano, civil rights movement was also making progress. There were efforts throughout the Southwest to demand equal rights for Mexican Americans.[63] Montejano credits "the demise of Jim Crow for Mexicans" with "fundamental shifts in economic and political conditions." [64] One part of that shift, as far as integrating the schools in Alpine, was an increase in the number of Mexican Americans and other progressives elected to office, particularly to the state level,[65] and a few at the local level. In the Sixty-First Texas Legislature in 1969, there were 11 Mexican Americans serving out of a total of 141 representatives, and there was one Mexican American in the state senate. Many of these newly elected Mexican American officials were dedicated to their community. And they were vocal.

One reason for this emerging political power was the effect of World War II. Returning veterans, using the G.I. Bill, had gone to college or trade schools, taking jobs with more stability and higher pay than they could have before their wartime service. World War II U.S. Navy veteran Alberto Rojo had grown up in nearby Marfa; he and his wife attended segregated schools there. "After World War II, we realized there was something else besides being segregated. I always fought for equality." [66] Rojo would join forces with other local parents to improve their children's education.

By the early 1960s these World War II–era veterans and their spouses were becoming community leaders. Joe Bernal, of San Antonio, became a state senator in 1966, the lone Mexican American in that body. Another elected official was Pete A. Gallego, an Alpine native son who had completed a business degree at Sul Ross State University and had chosen to stay in his hometown, to help his widowed mother in the family-owned restaurant, the popular Green Café. Gallego's wife, Elena Perez Gallego, of Fort Stockton, sixty-seven miles northeast, had also earned her degree at Sul Ross, and the two became civically involved. The couple had four children, and before long Gallego was volunteering as an election judge, making sure procedures were followed properly and earning the respect of his neighbors.

In 1959, the six-foot-one-inch, gangly Gallego was urged by local citizens to run for school board. He agreed. The Gallegos' own children attended the Anglo school and did well enough. But that was not the case for most Mexican American children, who stayed at Centennial.[67] There was nothing preventing the Mexican American children, per se, from going

FIGURE 1.6. *Alberto Rojo. Courtesy of the Voces Oral History Project.*

to the Anglo Central school, and yet, "You didn't want to go where . . . you had a feeling that they didn't want you around," Gallego said later.[68]

Few other Mexican American families in Alpine, though, had the temerity to cross over the tracks to attend Central. Instead, they wanted all Alpine's children to attend schools together; it was important that the Mexican American children not be treated as supplicants asking for better treatment at Central, the Anglo school, but rather they should feel that the school was *their* school, too. And Centennial would also be the school for all of them as well. Slowly, the idea gained steam. Something should be done. How?

Rojo, Gallego, and other concerned Mexican American parents began meeting, holding "powwows," trying to find a way to force integration on the town's schools. The meeting place, Rojo said later, was the Gallegos' Green Café. Alpine's problem came to the attention of Mexican Americans around the state. The G.I. Forum and LULAC offered to help, but Pete Gallego demurred. "I felt it was our own problem and to get somebody else would be a bigger problem . . . I thought then . . . 'I think we can do it. Give it time. And if not, I will later let you know. But I'll try to do it myself instead of getting too many people involved,'" he recalled.[69]

Gallego did correspond with Richard Avena, the Southwest Regional Director for the United States Civil Rights Commission, based in San Antonio. Gallego recalled that he drove twenty-five miles west to neighboring Marfa to post his letter to Avena, so that people in Alpine wouldn't know.[70] In the end, it was Alpine's Mexican American community, with the intervention of Mexican American legislators, that made the differ-

FIGURE 1.7. *Pete and Elena Gallego. Photo by James Evans. Courtesy of the Gallego family.*

ence. And the opening that presented itself was overcrowding. Alpine's schools needed more room.

THE SOLUTION

Texas Education Agency officials visited the schools in February 1969 and two months later told Alpine officials that if the overcrowding wasn't alleviated, the school's accreditation would be withdrawn as of July 1, 1970.[71] Alpine superintendent C. L. Winn told local parents that a loss of accreditation would mean a loss of sixty thousand dollars in salary aid from the state and that it would damage teacher morale and make it more difficult to recruit new teachers. Also, Alpine students seeking to transfer to another school would be required to take a placement test, a signal that there was a lack of confidence in what Alpine's schools were teaching. Loss of accreditation was a disaster to be avoided at all costs. A news story in the *Alpine Avalanche* said that the school board had met with the Alpine Chamber of Commerce and that a bond election would be held on May 3, less than two months away.[72]

Three bond proposals were offered to voters that May. The first was a tax to be imposed for routine maintenance. But it was the other two proposals that would determine whether the schools would be integrated:

- Proposition 2 would raise $1.5 million for a new high school, some remodels, and new classrooms. Most importantly, it called for the renovation of Centennial, the Mexican American school. That would mean the students would continue to be separated.
- Proposition 3 called for the sale of $800,000 in bonds to allow for placing all the elementary grades on one campus.[73]

The Mexican American parents endorsed Proposition 3, as it would force the integration of all students into one elementary school, one junior high, and one senior high school.

But in what the Mexican American community considered a betrayal, the Alpine Chamber of Commerce endorsed Proposition 2. The Chamber's decision only hardened the resolve of the Mexican American parents, and further polarized the town. That May, Proposition 2 passed 552 to 375. Proposition 3 failed: 479 voted against the proposal, 417 in favor. Rojo called the defeat of Proposition 3 "a bitter pill to swallow."[74]

The fight wasn't over. Over half of the Centennial parents immediately prepared a petition and presented it to the school board on May 13, saying that their children would be registered at Central. Rojo, representing a "Committee of Citizens for Better Schools," said that the 167 parent signatures represented 285 Centennial students. Rojo told the school board that the parents had worked alone, without any outside help.[75] But what Rojo didn't say was that patience was wearing thin; behind the scenes, the Mexican American community was weighing options, including seeking help from sympathetic state lawmakers.

There was one last attempt to settle the problem in-house. In July, trustee Pete Gallego proposed that the children in kindergarten through fourth grade go to Centennial and students in grades 5 to 8 would attend Central. The only other Mexican American on the school board, Johnny Sotello, seconded the proposal. Parents Alberto Rojo and Robert Garza appeared before the board, again endorsing the consolidation of the elementary grades.

But when Gallego's motion was put to a vote, the other four school board members rejected it. Then Johnny Sotello made a new proposal, one that confounded the Mexican American parents: he moved that the "open campus" policy be continued—meaning that elementary students could attend either Centennial or Central. Rojo and Garza knew that an open-campus policy would end any hope of integration; Anglo parents would never enroll their children at "the Mexican school." [76]

Undeterred with the three consecutive setbacks—the bond proposal defeat, the ignoring of the petition by Mexican American parents, and the school board rejection of the consolidation proposal—Gallego, Rojo, and the other parents contacted their legislators. Until then, the matter had been handled with neighborly civility. With the involvement of the elected officials from El Paso, that was about to change.

On July 15, 1969, State Representatives Paul Moreno (D-El Paso) and Raul Muñiz (D-El Paso), both members of the House Public Education Committee, drove to Alpine to meet with the Mexican American community. At the meeting, held at Our Lady of Peace Parish Hall, close to three hundred men and women listened to what the two elected officials had to say. Moreno told the gathering that segregated schools were unconstitutional—that the Supreme Court had repeatedly done away with segregation. Although the men served on the legislature's education committee, they said they had not been informed by the Texas Education Agency about Alpine's problems.[77] They wanted the other Mexican American legislators to hear about what was happening in Alpine. *Would the parents be willing to come to Austin to talk to the Mexican American legislators there?*

Within a week, on July 27, 1969, the caravan was on its way to Austin.

The Alpine group stayed overnight at an Austin hotel and met the following day with Texas Education Commissioner J. W. Edgar. The meeting was short. Board member Sotelo again seemed torn on the issue. He insisted on setting the record straight: he was invited to attend the Austin meeting as a private citizen and not as a trustee of the Alpine school board. He also said, according to Leyva and others at the meeting, that he saw "no problem" with separate schools—a statement that flummoxed the other parents.[78] The Mexican American legislators listened intently and promised to look into the matter. Within days, Alpine superintendent of schools Clarence L. Winn received a telegram from two of the legislators, Tati Santiesteban, and Paul Moreno, chairman and vice chairman, respectively, of the Mexican American delegation. The two asked Winn to meet with them at noon, August 11, 1969, in the old Texas supreme court chambers in Austin. The legislators had broadened the purpose of the meeting: besides the segregated schools, they also wanted to know why there wasn't a cafeteria at Centennial and why the May bond election had been held only at Central School rather than at Centennial as well. Winn acknowledged to a reporter that although Central had the only cafeteria, Centennial students who wished to use it were bused there. No cafeterias had been built at other schools because there wasn't enough space, he said. He also defended the use of Central as the site for the bond election, saying it had been used over the last couple of years.[79]

At the August 11 meeting with the legislators, Superintendent Winn read a ten-page report on the background of Alpine Schools: the new high school would house grades 9–12; grades 7 and 8 would be in the present high school; all elementary pupils would be on the Central School campus "after 16 new classrooms are constructed, to be finished by September 1970. Centennial could be used for area vocational classes." The mood was tense.

Bernal told Winn that he was "put out that 27 people have to come 450 miles to complain to the state legislature about a situation that has many ramifications. What would be the reason if not prejudice and discrimination? There must be a feeling they couldn't communicate with you and the board president or they were pretty stupid."

Winn replied: "We did not come to debate with you. You asked for a report, and we gave it to you." [80]

One senator, W. E. "Pete" Snelson (D-Midland), who was not a member of the Mexican American delegation, but whose district included Alpine, accused Bernal of grandstanding. "We are in no position to badger these people," Snelson said. "This line of questioning indicates to me that you are more interested in publicity than anything else." Bernal retorted that he saw nothing wrong in openly discussing "injustices." State Representative Paul Moreno was more forceful: "I am not here for publicity. I am sick and tired of discrimination against Mexican-Americans. I will do anything in my power to help prevent it. We have been stepped on and stomped on. It irritates the hell out of you. This is something very emotional to us."

Winn told the legislators that plans were adopted by the Alpine school board on July 30 that would consolidate the schools. "While prejudice probably did initially dictate the dual elementary school plan, the present school board is anxious to remedy the problem in the most equitable manner possible," the school plan said.

The plan would consolidate the first four grades on one campus, the second four grades on another, and senior high school on the third.

Elena Gallego said that the school district's plans were "fine . . . if carried out." She told a reporter that she would like to see the consolidation put into effect immediately. Her husband, board member Pete Gallego, also noted that within Alpine's Mexican American community, many were unconvinced that the plan would be implemented.[81]

Alpine's Mexican Americans would not leave the integration to chance, or to the goodwill of the school officials. "Since the people had been roused and everything . . . by the state representatives that came to speak to the people . . . we called them [community members] together and we said, 'Well, the only way that we can now integrate is, if they don't want to do it any other way, we're going to force it,'" Elena Gallego said years later. The strategy was simple, the Gallegos told their neighbors: "'Y'all just go ahead and register your kids on the other [Anglo] side and don't register anybody on the Mexican side.' . . . They [the opponents] never thought that we would simply get out en masse."[82]

When enrollment opened for the 1969 school year, the Mexican American parents took their sons and daughters to Central. Winn reported that, with registration about 90 percent complete, 621 students had registered at Central and only 123 enrolled at Centennial. There were only forty-five children in Centennial's grades six through eight; it was clearly unfeasible to offer a junior high curriculum to so few students. On August 15, 1969, with the knowledge that a small but powerful group of politicians would be watching, the Alpine school board voted to consolidate Central and Centennial.[83] Consolidation passed 6–1.[84]

It had taken caravans, bond proposals, petitions, meetings, and more meetings. But it was finally the simple act of the Mexican American parents registering their children at the Anglo school—while keeping Mexican American elected officials apprised of their actions—that integrated Alpine public schools.

The fallout from the integration battle fell hard on some. The Green Café, the Gallego family business, was boycotted; on one day, it made less than five dollars. The Gallegos moved the restaurant to another location, north of the tracks, across the street from Sul Ross. The college crowd kept the business afloat, and in time it was thriving again.

Elidia Leyva wondered how her political involvement would affect her job at Forchheimer's Department Store, where she worked with her cousin.

> *Yo y mi otra amiga, prima, trabajábamos allí y . . . las dos pedimos permiso a ir [to Austin] y creíamos que no nos iban a dar permiso porque uno de los dueños estaba en el* school board *y ya él sabía lo que* was going on *y lo que estabamos haciendo y creamos no nos iban a dar. Pero si nos dieron permiso. Pero al mismo tiempo decíamos nosotros que, "Chansa que cuando vuelvanos pa' tras no vamos a tener trabajo, nos van a correr." Pero nunca nos dijeron nada.*

> [Me and my other friend, a cousin, worked there and . . . both of us asked permission to go (to Austin), and we thought that they weren't going to give us permission because one of the owners was on the school board, and he knew what was going on and what we were doing and we thought that they weren't going to (give permission). But they did give it to us. At the same time, we thought, "Maybe when we get back, we aren't going to have a job; they're going to fire us." But they never said anything.]

It was a difficult adjustment for some Anglos. On September 1, 1969, the school trustees called a special meeting to hear complaints from a new group, Concerned Citizens for School Improvements. The chairman of the group said the parents' concern was the "welfare both academically and physically of all the children," according the *Alpine Avalanche*. The meeting went for an hour and a half. The group asked that "complete press coverage be employed during the meeting," apparently to counter the press attention that had been given to the Mexican American parent group. One concern was the safety of children crossing the railroad tracks, to which Alberto Rojo shot back: "Now you know how we feel!" [85]

A news story about the meeting says that Superintendent Winn and board members answered questions and tried to assure the parents that their children would receive "the best it has ever been." After the meeting, Causey said she was still worried about transportation. Board president Bob Halpern said the board would discuss the matter at a later date.[86]

That day never came. Instead, the Alpine schools remained integrated.

The new group, opposed to the integration, lacked the determination and persistence of the group of Mexican Americans who one summer day in August 1969 packed bologna and cheese sandwiches, climbed into a caravan of cars, and drove 450 miles to their state capitol to plead with state officials for their children's education.

TWO

The Multistep Integration of the El Paso Police Department

In the spring of 1960, the attorney Albert Armendariz took a seat at a table with seven other men for his first meeting of the El Paso Civil Service Commissioners.[1] Armendariz was civically active: a private practice attorney and a leader at both the community and the national level. But in this arena, he was simply a citizen, serving as an appointee of Mayor Raymond L. Telles, the first Hispanic mayor of this westernmost Texas city. The agenda at this meeting included the approval of the eligibility lists of applicants for the city's police and fire departments. Armendariz immediately zeroed in on a problem. *Why were the Spanish-surnamed applicants crossed out in red ink?*[2]

His question, and the investigation that followed, would be the first in a sequence of events that would integrate El Paso's police and fire departments. A similar chapter on the integration of the public safety forces could have been written about many other cities and towns in Texas, and indeed across the Southwest, because in 1960, there was a widespread practice of excluding minorities. Lawsuits offered one strategy for challenging the practice. In Houston, Mexican Americans were galvanized to demand equal treatment in a public meeting with the police chief in 1953.[3] El Paso, however, is a particularly interesting case: its public safety integration was achieved by the city's first Hispanic mayor circumventing his own political limitations and strategizing to effect the change.

World War II–era veterans often led the way. Many involved in the integration had lost any prewar timidity to challenge authority; they felt entitled to equal treatment. Armendariz, for instance, had served in the U.S. Army, stationed at Fort Bliss, outside of El Paso. His military job was to supervise the motor pool. "I was in charge of 350 vehicles and as many employees," he said. "I told captains what to do; I assigned vehicles to generals. I wasn't the same person before the Army experience that I am sitting here today," he said in a 1992 interview.[4]

Raymond Telles's election had much to do with Raymond Telles's stature as a "clean" candidate: a decorated military veteran from a sturdy middle-class background, a graduate of El Paso's best Catholic schools, a business school education, a sterling job record, the father of young children. In short, he was, in many respects, the All-American candidate, appealing to a broad public. This chapter is about how a Mexican American elected official in the 1960s cautiously navigated the political landscape of this border town to integrate its police and fire departments. And it is about an equality of opportunity that eluded Mexican American job seekers, even in the public sector.

The backdrop is a city with powerful and moneyed—and mostly Anglo—interests who had been accustomed to a deciding role in the future of their city. Left out of the discussion had been the Mexican-descent population and others who rejected the idea of a minority of elites ruling over them. On both sides of the border, Telles's 1957 election was celebrated: *it could be done after all.* And that "it" was that Mexican Americans could promote their own, elect their own, see their own in important posts.

EL PASO

In the late 1950s El Paso, the state's westernmost city, was around 50 percent Mexican American.[5] It enjoyed a confluence of favorable elements: its geographic location on the Rio Grande offered a "Pass to the North" between what would become Mexico and the United States. Originally home to Native Americans, in the late sixteenth century Spaniards arrived, some settling on either side of the river, others passing through to points northward. In 1881, with the arrival of the Southern Pacific Railroad (now known as the Southern Pacific Transportation Company), El Paso became a crossroads for trade.[6] During and after the Mexican Revolution, which began in 1910 and lasted for the better part of a decade, El Paso's population burgeoned with Mexican immigrants escaping the chaos and violence. Those same immigrants—some intellectuals and political dissidents fleeing repression and a larger number of displaced laborers who had lost their land through government policies and were looking for jobs—swelled the Mexican population of El Paso.[7]

But while their numbers were substantial, they had no voice. In the first two decades of the twentieth century, a small group of El Paso Anglo Democrats, known as "the Ring," held fast to political power. Mexican American ward heelers delivered Mexican American voters to Ring candidates in exchange for political influence.[8] But the power of those Mexican American politicos was severely limited: they could enjoy some favors, but the benefits did not extend to the larger Mexican American community. They could not, for example, improve the substandard housing where thousands of families lived on the crowded Segundo Barrio, or Second Ward. And there was little they would do to fund the ill-equipped public schools that most of the Mexican American children attended. The Ring disbanded after 1916, when it was successfully challenged. But during its day, it had contributed to "a pattern of political manipulation, subordination, and underrepresentation . . . in the border city and throughout much of the Southwest."[9] Once that template was in place, it could be replicated, but it would be difficult to replace.

THE ELECTION OF RAYMOND L. TELLES

Raymond Telles's father, Ramón—or Don Ramón, as he was known in the Mexican Southside—was involved in El Paso politics during the 1930s, heading what Telles would later describe as an informal political organization. Don Ramón delivered the Southside vote to candidates who promised to improve conditions in the impoverished area, Raymond Telles would say later.[10] By the mid- to late 1950s, El Paso's business leaders, dubbed "the Kingmakers" by an irreverent local newspaper editor, were accustomed to determining and controlling city leadership. Mexican Americans, who made up about half of the population, were largely excluded: a lack of elected Mexican American officials was one of the clearest indications of "second-class citizenship."[11] That would remain true for the following decades. For instance, there were only two Mexican Americans among Texas's twenty-three Congressmen serving from 1960 through 1970, after the state gained one more seat.[12] In 1960, only three Mexican Americans served in the 150-seat state house and only one served in the state senate.

The lack of Mexican American political representation was true not only for Texas but also throughout the Southwest. In 1960 California had only five Mexican American state assemblymen (the equivalent of the Texas House) and no Mexican American state senators.[13] In 1960, the U.S.

city with the largest Mexican American population, Los Angeles, had no Mexican Americans on its city council. Not that the Mexican American community had been passive; in fact, the political scientist Rodolph O. de la Garza notes that there had been a long tradition of Mexican American involvement in mainstream politics, most notably in the 1938 presidential election of Franklin D. Roosevelt. FDR's immigration policies had met with the approval of the Mexican American electorate and had engendered a few generations of Democratic-leaning Mexican Americans. The postwar urbanization of the general population, including Mexican Americans, and the access to educational opportunities afforded by the G.I. Bill provided an opening for greater political representation. Holding political office would be a natural progression.

World War II–era veteran Raymond Telles returned to his hometown of El Paso in 1947, after serving in the U.S. Air Force as head of the Latin American Division, which provided equipment and training to Latin American countries. He had seen some of the world, had managed men, and had proven himself. To his father and politically involved younger brother, Richard, Raymond Telles had taken on the aura of a contender. His credentials were considered impeccable: he had graduated from a good Catholic high school, the prestigious Cathedral; finished business school; worked for the Workers' Progress Administration as a bookkeeper; and then worked as an accountant for the federal penitentiary in La Tuna, in Anthony, Texas, twenty miles north of El Paso. Telles had excelled in the military.

> Having gone in as a buck private and come out as a major — they felt
> that that was important and that maybe I should attempt to break the
> ice . . . in the sense that he and his friends felt that it was time that
> we as a group [speaking again of the Spanish-surnamed American —
> Mexicans or Chicanos] . . . that we became more directly involved
> in the political life of our community of our county and state and so
> forth. . . . My father, along with a few of his friends, suggested to me
> that I should run for County Clerk of El Paso County. I wasn't interested in politics and so I just actually refused to do so. This went on for
> a number of months, I guess. . . . Anyway, my father and his friends
> kept insisting. At one point I felt that in some way I had more or less
> hurt my father's feelings — not only in his own concept, or idea that we
> should become involved; that we should care about what happened to
> our Mexican Americans[,] Mexican Americans political, economy and
> social situation of our people.[14]

FIGURE 2.1. *Raymond*
Telles. Courtesy of the
University of Texas at El Paso
Library, Special Collections
Department, El Paso Herald-
Post *Records, MS 348.*

Telles's father and brother recognized that military veterans were more attractive political candidates. Veteran status has always been a selling point for contenders to public office. Military experience affords expanded horizons, resources, and opportunities the veteran might not otherwise have enjoyed. The military may lead individuals to reevaluate themselves, and their potential; it might inspire within them an internal drive that makes political involvement a possibility they might not have otherwise entertained.[15] For minorities, it may also be that military service is a type of "bridging environment" that allows for greater integration into the dominant society—exposing them to the bureaucracy and discipline that they may apply later to other systems.[16] Employers, in particular, may attach special significance to military service and use veteran status as one way to filter out the most attractive job applicants—an interpretation that surely could be extended to how voters might perceive political candidates.

For Mexican American World War II veterans, military service also signified a duty met. They had demonstrated their allegiance to their country and would not tolerate suggestions to the contrary—in fact, others outside of their ethnic group may also defend them.[17] In general, contenders for public office who are military veterans enjoy a certain allure.[18]

Finally, Latino World War II veterans were especially ready to claim their rights.

"I credit World War II with making us aware of the other side of the coin," Armendariz said in 1992. "For instance, we got into a jeep, drove a jeep, when many of us had never gotten into a car. We got into office jobs and were given the right to do that. We got behind a gun and were given the responsibility of shooting. As a society, we had never been given the opportunity of doing something and succeeding at it."[19]

Where some men may have been self-directed to seek public office, others, like Telles, were pressured by relatives and friends.[20] After several months of considering it, in 1948 Telles relented and agreed to run for El Paso County Clerk, with little expectation of winning.[21] The obstacles were obvious: El Paso's Mexican American voting population was small, made even smaller by the $1.75 annual poll tax required of all voters.[22] "The people in the south part of town [with the heaviest concentrations of Mexican Americans] did well to keep body and soul together, much less go out and splurge on paying for a poll tax," Telles said.[23] Undeterred, Telles's father and brother and other supporters launched an aggressive get-out-the-vote campaign that was intertwined with the Telles County Clerk effort. The campaign held dances, raffles, even collected donations from businessmen friends of Richard Telles's in Ciudad Juárez, across the border.[24]

Race played a role in the campaign. The incumbent, El Paso County Clerk P. D. Lowry, who had been in office since 1938, underscored the racial difference in radio presentations: "I want the people of El Paso to know two things about me and my opposition. First of all, his name is *Ramón Telles*. And my name is P. D. Lowry. He's a Mexican and I'm Scotch-Irish." [25] Lowry apparently misread both the potential and determination of the Mexican American electorate, as well Telles's Anglo supporters. In the end, Telles managed to squeak by with a 563 vote margin: 9,341 to 8,778.[26] Although Telles won overwhelmingly in the largely Mexican American precincts, he also did well in areas of El Paso that were predominantly Anglo, affirming his belief that he could not win an election without Anglo support. His opponent cast doubt on the heavily Mexican American precincts: "I was defeated by the Spanish American vote. It seems peculiar that at San Elizario [Pct. 47], I should get only 9 votes where I had at least five workers there and in Pct. 1 [Alamo School] I should get only 23 of the 623 cast. However I am not contesting. I am not a crybaby." [27]

Telles proved a capable county clerk, and was reelected—unopposed—four more times.[28] In 1957, after repeated urging by supporters, Telles raised his sights to the much-higher-profile post of mayor. He would challenge the shorter-term incumbent, the businessman Tom Rogers, who had been appointed to fill out the term of a mayor who had fallen ill immediately after his election. Armendariz and others felt that, with Telles, Mexican Americans finally had their chance: "Our leadership had been told time after time that the reason we didn't go up was because we weren't qualified. And this was a term that was not only used against us, but it hurt. It ruffled our dignity as a group. It was a system . . . a modus operandi: 'You're not qualified.' And in doing this [campaigning] for Raymond, we were able to . . . present an entirely qualified candidate." [29]

Armendariz and other volunteers knew that Telles would need the Anglos, most of whom were excluded from the Kingmaker circles. The Telles camp assembled a "People's Ticket," a slate that included, besides Telles as mayor, four unproven Anglo candidates to the city council: one was an insurance agent, another a car dealer, another a broadcast weatherman, and the fourth a businessman. Telles told local reporters that if voters elected the People's Ticket, "we will have a successful administration of the people, by the people and for the people. . . . We shall bow to no bosses." [30] Observers could see that Telles's candidacy in 1957 would be the first time that Mexican Americans could be said to have acted "independently of the dominant business-professional coalition." [31]

The Telles campaign machine worked vigorously and their slate won the nomination soundly: 18,688 to the incumbent Tom Rogers's 15,934.[32]

El Paso, in 1957, was Democratic country, as was the rest of Texas. When city candidates won their party's nomination in the city's Democratic primary, they were guaranteed a win: there was no Republican Party to speak of. The Democratic nominees were the winners—no general election necessary. Telles had won the party's nomination and was thus the presumptive mayor-elect. In any other year and with any other candidate, that would have been the case. But this was 1957, and Telles had challenged the Kingmakers who had not approved of Telles's candidacy. In a surprise move, after the primary, an unanticipated write-in candidate emerged, a move that would require a general election.

The write-in candidate was a little-known former deputy superintendent in the El Paso Independent School District, M. R. Hollenshead.

FIGURE 2.2. *Albert Armendariz. Courtesy of the Voces Oral History Project.*

Liberal *El Paso Herald-Post* editor Ed Pooley and the Spanish-language newspaper, *El Continental*, decried the write-in campaign as racist, particularly coming at the last minute, only after Telles had won the Democratic primary. Pooley called the move one of "bigotry and prejudice" and *El Continental* said it was "discriminatory, anti-Latin and—why not say it—anti-Catholic."[33] But the *El Paso Times*, which had endorsed the incumbent Rogers, supported the write-in process: "All that a primary can do is say that it is the will of those who participated in that primary to 'nominate' this or that candidate who will represent that party in the general election," the newspaper's editorial said. The editorial also said that it was possible that some people had erroneously voted for the wrong candidate in the primary; the general election would provide those voters with the chance of casting their vote for the mayoral candidate they wanted.[34]

Telles's campaign rallied—energized by the obvious attempt to subvert the Democratic primary and overturn Telles's victory. But if Telles's opponent expected all Anglos to fall in behind a fellow Anglo, they had miscalculated. Two months later, Telles won by a landslide: 17,080 to 8,961, carrying the precincts in the predominantly Mexican American areas of town, as well as Anglo precincts, suggesting that those voters, too, saw through the ploy.[35] When Telles took office on April 11, 1957, *El Continental* proclaimed in its headline: "Telles, Alcalde Paisano."[36]

ALBERT ARMENDARIZ

Telles had found a loyal public servant in Albert Armendariz. The son of Mexican immigrants who came to El Paso before Albert was born in 1919, Armendariz attended the racially mixed schools "north of the tracks." His parents were determined that their children's English would be good and that their education was the best they could obtain. Armendariz graduated from El Paso High, a mixed-race school, in 1939 and then worked as a salesman at the Lion Shoe Store. But he had noticed a disturbing pattern at the store. Mexican American salesmen, regardless of how successful and intelligent, were not promoted to managerial positions. Instead the owner would bring in Anglos with less experience. He moved to a civilian position at Fort Bliss, working in the motor pool, readying trucks to be put on flatbeds. Armendariz was drafted in the spring of 1943 and served stateside at Fort Bliss, in El Paso, during World War II. His position as head of the motor pool gave him an idea of his abilities. So it was that after the war, as a civilian, he applied for an administrative job at Fort Bliss. He was turned down and was told that the base had chosen another man, an Anglo, because the other man had one year of college. Armendariz didn't buy the explanation. But that rejection had a profound effect on him: he would get a college degree; no one would ever be able to use *that* excuse again. It would have another effect on him, too. He would use that sense of fairness in employment on the Civil Service Commission.

With his forty months of G.I. Bill educational benefits, Armendariz attended UT–El Paso and then graduated from the prestigious University of Southern California Law School. It had not been an easy progression. In law school, he felt initially marginalized by his cohort and sought solace from his wife, Mary Lou, whom he had married right after high school. "When I'd come home complaining to my wife, she'd bawl me out and say, 'You're not here to make friends; you're here to become a lawyer,'" Armendariz recalled.[37] Armendariz was active in Mexican American organizations, and served as national president of the League of United Latin American Citizens (LULAC) in 1953. He would be the first chairman of the board of the Mexican American Legal Defense and Educational Fund (MALDEF), in 1969. Later, he would be appointed as a federal immigration judge by President Jimmy Carter. After Mary Lou's death in 1993, he married Mari de Jesus Jauregui.

Well into his seventies, Armendariz continued to practice law, representing undocumented immigrant clients in the small West Texas towns, with Mari at the wheel of the car. Hard of hearing, he frustrated a judge in one courtroom who impatiently advised the white-haired Armendariz that it was time for him to retire. "No one's going to tell me when to retire!" an indignant Armendariz recounted later.[38]

In fact, Armendariz's ability to stand his ground would serve him well on the El Paso City Civil Service Commission. Telles would count on Armendariz's steadfastness to address the lack of Mexican American city employers. That moment arrived when Armendariz and his fellow commissioners reviewed the eligibility lists of the police and fire departments.

CIVIL SERVICE

Telles had appointed Armendariz in April 1960.[39] It was not a glamorous assignment, but it was powerful, overseeing the city's employees. Civil service jobs were a gateway into secure employment, with the possibility of regular raises and opportunities for promotion. To safeguard the integrity of that civil service employment system, the civil service commissioners attended to the tedious technical details involving pay grades. Later, human resources officers would take over the more routine daily tasks, like approving sick leave as reflected in the civil service meeting records. But in 1960, Armendariz and his fellow commissioners oversaw it all: the incremental steps to reach the next pay grades, requests from city employees to accept outside employment, employee dismissals, and waivers of physical qualifications for certain jobs.[40] In essence, they oversaw the city employee ranks for this city of 250,000.

For applicants, the public sector jobs represented more than steady employment—although that was important. These city jobs were one of the few avenues to reaching middle-class income, having the opportunity to be judged on merit, and receiving regular promotions and good benefits. That, at least, was the ideal. The commission was authorized to intervene, to hold departments accountable and ensure equitability. It was obvious to any observant person glancing over the lists of city employees, or even walking into a city office, that Spanish-surnamed employees were concentrated in the lower-paying jobs—maintenance and janitorial positions.[41] Few were in the white-collar or supervisory ranks. Although Mayor Telles was aware of the disparity, he was also wary of taking too public a stance on the issue. He could not afford to alienate the Anglo voters who helped elect him. Instead, he equalized opportunities quietly, appointing individuals like Armendariz, who could make the appropriate challenges. Telles's instructions for Armendariz were to lead the way.

[Telles] told me he was not going to be able to back me. That he wanted me to know this because "I [Telles] have to assume the character of a mayor for everybody. But I'm putting you in there because I know there's a lot of problems with city employment. And I want you to see what you can do about 'em. But I want you to know you're on your own. . . . I'm putting you in there because you have the ability to do it without my help." He wasn't going to actively back me.[42]

Civil service jobs have been used as currency within the U.S. political landscape since the nation's earliest days, with city employment rooted in a federal counterpart. Early government jobs were part of a spoils system, distributed as a reward for campaign contributions and other favors.[43] In a nineteenth-century system that called for "political assessments," the employee was required to financially support his political party so that it could maintain power and the employee could thereby keep his job. Corruption became especially rampant after the Civil War, when the numbers of federal appointees grew by 173 percent in the twenty years between 1861 and 1881.[44] When Charles Guiteau, "a disappointed office-seeker," fatally shot President James A. Garfield in 1881, the inherent corruption of the federal jobs program became a national news story; Americans became committed to reforming the spoils system.[45] In 1883, Congress passed the Pendleton Civil Service Reform Act, which required, among other things, that job seekers pass exams before being hired under a merit system.[46]

Despite the reforms, the civil service system did not provide equal opportunity for all job seekers. As evidence, one could look at the 1966 employment of Mexican Americans in federal civil service jobs, which this chapter will consider shortly. The World War II generation of Latinos was keenly aware of the discrimination against them at all levels. As with Armendariz, it had happened to them. And they knew that if private employers couldn't be required to be fair, governmental institutions should ensure equal opportunity. This issue of public jobs was both a symptom and a contributor to the inequalities faced by Mexican Americans throughout the Southwest. Mexican Americans were grossly underrepresented in government jobs at all levels, including the oldest and largest one—the federal post office. For African Americans, on the other hand, the U.S. Postal Service had been a safe haven since almost the start of the agency. Historians can trace postal employment among African Americans from as early as 1869, in New Bedford, Massachusetts.[47] And after Reconstruction, postal jobs opened up for more African Americans. Public sector jobs were key to the development of a black middle class, allowing the individual postal worker a chance to earn higher wages, as well as creating avenues for collective bargaining and for civic involvement. It was such a reliable source of jobs for African Americans that "There's always room at the post office!" became a catchphrase in the 1987 movie *Hollywood Shuffle*. Many successful African Americans, or their parents or grandparents, worked for the post office.[48]

For Mexican Americans, the post office did not represent the same easy access. There is evidence of Mexican Americans serving as postmasters in small, isolated communities before World War II.[49] But there were many instances well after World War II of Mexican Americans being shut out of these jobs.[50]

Civil service employment was one of many areas of job discrimination that riled Mexican American political activists: taxpayer money was being used to discriminate against them. Alfred J. Hernandez, an attorney, Houston municipal judge, and the national president of LULAC in 1965, reported on the underrepresentation, basing his testimony on the 1966 statistics from the U.S. Civil Service Commission.[51] Hernandez gave a blistering accounting of the federal government's failure to employ Mexican Americans. There was abundant evidence that Spanish-surnamed Americans were underrepresented in federal civil service jobs—and even more so in the ranks of decision-making or supervisory positions. Hernandez noted that in cases where a department had aggressively sought to address the underrepresentation, it had succeeded:

> In the last two months, this Department [of Agriculture] has embarked upon a bold and aggressive program of affirmative action . . . and during this period has succeeded in employing 326 Americans of Spanish surnames. It is evident, therefore, that whenever a Department determines that it is going to seek out qualified minority group applicants, it can find them. . . . It must be made clear to all government agencies that the worn out statement and tired phrase, "We do not have more employees of Spanish surname because there just aren't any qualified," is no longer acceptable to our group.[52]

Hernandez noted that poor Mexican Americans were being underserved by departments charged with helping them. For instance, the Department of Labor had not established a solid presence among the Latino community. Its solution for job training for Mexican Americans was for positions that either required little actual training or offered little chance for advancement: gas station attendants, short-order cooks, and television repairmen.[53]

FIGURE 2.3. *Alfred J. Hernandez. Courtesy of the Voces Oral History Project.*

In some cases, the federal government agencies' efforts defied logic: the Immigration and Naturalization Service and the Border Patrol invested money in teaching Spanish to non-Spanish-speaking recruits—a requirement for the job—at their training facility in Port Isabel, Texas. The more practical solution would have been to concentrate efforts on recruiting and training Mexican Americans who were already bilingual, he said. Hernandez gave the example of one El Paso employee of the Department of Justice who held the rank of a GS-4 but had the job responsibilities of interpreter, which was at the higher GS 7–9 rank. "She is held responsible for this most delicate and vital work, yet she is not considered to be qualified for a promotion to a GS-5," he said.[54]

Hernandez noted the irony that the department charged with helping to "eliminate poverty" had only scant Hispanic representation in its ranks. And he turned his attention to the federal Civil Service Commission—the very agency he was testifying before and the one charged with overseeing the progress of federal employment. He noted that the information he was using for his own report came from a 1966 study of racial and ethnic employment in the federal government. But while 150 pages of the report were dedicated to issues surrounding African Americans, only 14 pages focused on problems of Mexican Americans and only 12 spotlighted problems of Native Americans. "It is important that we begin our study with the agency that compiled this report—the Civil Service Commission," he said.[55]

Hernandez said there had never been a Spanish-surnamed person among the three-person panel of civil service commissioners. The panel immediately below the commission, the Board of Appeals and Reviews, "whose primary function is to pass upon all appeals brought forth from civil service employees who feel that their rights have been violated by their supervisors in either promotions or terminations," also had no Mexican Americans. At the regional levels, there were no Mexican American directors, to his knowledge, and only a few Mexican American investigators, whose duties included "investigating alleged complaints of discrimination in government agencies and military installations."[56]

"If the Civil Service Commission is to be charged with the responsibility of enforcing the provisions of nondiscrimination in employment, promotions, transfers, and terminations in all government agencies, it must set the example and enforce these provisions within its own system," Hernandez said.[57]

Hernandez and other civil rights advocates knew that the simple

TABLE 2.1. HISPANIC FEDERAL EMPLOYMENT, 1966

Department	Number of Employees	Percent Spanish surnamed	Percent Spanish surnamed at higher ranks
Labor	9,626	0.9	1.0
Housing and Urban Development	14,057	0.8	NA
Health, Education and Welfare	90,695	1.3	0.8
Agriculture	102,184	1.6	0.4
Office of Economic Opportunity	2,637	1.9	
Justice*	32,960	1.6	0.5
Defense	1,024,048	3.8	6.9

Source: *The Mexican American: A New Focus on Opportunity*. Testimony presented at the Cabinet Committee Hearings on Mexican American Affairs, Inter-Agency Committee on Mexican American Affairs, El Paso, Texas, October 26–28, 1967.

* Included the then separate agencies of the Immigration and Naturalization Service and the Border Patrol.

passing of a law did not guarantee its enforcement. Rather, the passage required a political process to ensure the law's success.[58] That process could include lawsuits, internal and external pressure, and the public acceptance of the practice. Civil rights advocates knew that at any point the law could be circumvented.[59] If individuals in positions of effecting equality of opportunity were not supportive of equal opportunity, then it was unlikely that the jobs would be opened to minorities and others.

In El Paso, the process integrating the police and fire departments required several steps: poll taxes were paid; the voters turned out to elect Telles; and he found a quiet way to bring greater equality to municipal government. Each step hinged on the successful completion of the previous step. Each step required dispensing with an "old" way of doing things and the embracing of new thinking, new approaches, and an underlying belief among Mexican Americans and their supporters that, indeed, it was possible to bring Mexican Americans into a fuller participation in their city.

So, in April 1960, Armendariz stared down at the list of police and firefighter candidates. These were the men (all men) who had already passed a written test, Armendariz recalled in a 1992 interview.

The theory of civil service is that if a department asks for one officer, you give him the top three and he chooses from the top three and
the others go to the top of the line.

[The list] passed through every commissioner without comment,
not one word. . . . I looked at this list and every Hispanic name on
those lists was red-lined, had a red line through it. And it says d-e-p-t-
period r-e-f period. Every Hispanic name. Not one Hispanic name was
not red-lined. I glanced at it and asked, "What is this, Mr. Adair?"

[Adair, the civil service commission chair, responded] "What do
you mean, Mr. Armendariz?"

"What is this redline and what does this d-e-p-t- period r-e-f
mean?" And he says—he doesn't answer my question—he says, "Well,
we can't tell them who to hire." And I said, "Well, Mr. Adair, you amaze
me: what are we doing here, if we're the civil service? Are these our
lists? Or are they somebody else's list?"

[Adair responded] "No, they're our lists." [Armendariz responded]
". . . Well, why do you say that we can't tell them who? We're the ones
who make these lists, don't we?" Adair came back quickly: "Are you
alleging discrimination?" Jumped on it. And I said, "Thou has said it—
that's what it looks like to me." And then he did something that I never,
never expected and I'll always be grateful to him for. He says, "Mr.
Armendariz, in view of the charges you made, I'm going to name you
a committee of one. I'm going to table until the next meeting"—it's a
monthly meeting—"And I'm going to ask you to report in writing."

Armendariz was given access to the fire and police department files
and spent a week investigating, scrutinizing every folder of a Spanish-
surnamed applicant. He found that in the ten-year period before the
meeting, every Hispanic applicant had been redlined in both the fire and
the police departments. In some cases, non-Spanish-surnamed applicants
who had been redlined either had a Mexican wife or a Mexican mother.
"It was that deep-rooted that they would look at the man's mother," said
Armendariz.

The same process was happening for African American applicants—
if it could be ascertained by their address that they were not white, they,
too, were redlined.

He knew there were some Mexican American police officers, so, he
wondered, *why had they been hired?* "So I went back into the archives and
[looked up] Islas, Carreon—I remember their names because they were
so few of them—all of them had an excuse, written excuse in the file: "'I

need him for liaison with the Juárez Police Department, or the Juárez Fire Department.' . . . 'I need a Spanish-speaker for downtown patrol.' They had to give a special reason why they hired a Mexican," Armendariz said.[60]

Armendariz reported his findings to the commission and proposed a new policy statement: all applicants would be scrutinized by the Civil Service Commission; department heads no longer had the authority to summarily rule out applicants. In cases in which a department head had reason to drop a candidate from consideration after the commission had approved him, the department head would be required to state the reason in writing, and there would be a hearing with the applicant in an effort to have his voice heard.

"The commission accepted those [guidelines] immediately, no comment. Move to accept, accept. And the issue was dead," Armendariz said. "And we opened up the police department and the fire department to Hispanics. Now we have a Hispanic chief of police." [61]

The changes instituted by the El Paso Civil Service Commission required some vigilance. Once the equal treatment was accepted, the entire commission appears to have upheld the policy: Anglo commissioners sided with the Mexican Americans who had been arbitrarily removed from eligibility lists. In one 1963 case, the El Paso Fire Chief removed two Spanish-surnamed individuals from the eligibility lists, one for an "Attitude of indifference," and the other for being "unable to follow instructions." The new commission chair, James Malone, called those reasons "marginal" and said that the names "should have been submitted to the Commission prior to the completion of all additional tests."

The commission agreed to remind both the police and the fire chiefs that "arbitrary removal of names from the eligible lists, after all parts of the examinations have been completed and passed, will not be condoned or approved . . . no removals will be made on an arbitrary or superficial basis." [62]

It would not only be Mexican Americans endorsing fairness in the city's public jobs.

EPILOGUE

Telles won an unopposed race in 1959. Two years later, after he had announced his candidacy for a third term, he was recruited by President John F. Kennedy to serve as ambassador to Costa Rica.[63] Although Telles was reluctant to leave his hometown — he knew he would have been unopposed in the next election—he was finally swayed when Kennedy told him he was being selfish: Telles would be the country's first Spanish-surnamed ambassador. Telles would be opening the door for future Mexican Americans to serve in other diplomatic posts.[64] The Telles family moved to Costa Rica, and Telles served as ambassador for six years. Following that, he served in various federal positions in Washington, D.C., and El Paso.[65]

After being away from El Paso for a decade, Telles came home hungry for another elected office. He trained his sights on the Sixteenth Congressional District, occupied by Richard White. Telles and his younger brother Richard sought to recapture the 1957 energy and excitement. But Telles found he had been away too long, had been out of the public eye too long. He lost decisively.[66] Some critics would say that his style of leadership wasn't as bold as the 1960 generation of Mexican Americans—many calling themselves Chicanas and Chicanos—expected of their leaders.

Critics would later say that Telles could have had a greater and more long-lasting impact had he remained in El Paso and groomed more Mexican Americans to take leadership positions.[67] But at the time, Telles faced pressure from many. Left alone, he may have been happy serving as county clerk until he retired, or even working as an accountant at the federal penitentiary. But for his time, Telles was one of the few Mexican Americans in El Paso who could, or who would agree to, take on the Kingmakers, to balance the many interests without alienating his base. Even the president of the United States persuaded him to serve as an ambassador.

Today, both the El Paso Police Department and the El Paso Fire Department are three-quarters Hispanic.[68] Raymond Telles and his appointee Albert Armendariz found a way to take the steps so that the city's two public service departments could more nearly reflect their local population.

PART 2

Claiming Rights on a National Level

THREE

MALDEF: *Born into the Crosswinds of the Chicano Movement*

By the mid-1960s, there had been a string of court cases touching on issues of jury discrimination against African Americans and Mexican Americans. Time and again, attorneys representing minority clients had complained to judges that their clients were entitled to juries of their *peers*—and that meant, for Mexican Americans in the Southwest in particular, other Mexican Americans. While not a constitutional right—the Sixth Amendment only specifies an "impartial" jury—the courts had repeatedly interpreted impartiality to require that the juries include men and women who physically resembled those seeking justice.[1] And the issue of jury selection as it affected Mexican Americans was at the heart of the 1954 landmark *Hernandez v. Texas*, in which the Supreme Court had recognized Mexican Americans as "a class apart."[2]

And yet, here was attorney Pete Tijerina on a hot June day in 1966, reviewing the list of potential jurors in a courtroom in Jourdanton, county seat of Atascosa County in South Texas. There was not a single Spanish surname on the list. Tijerina's client, a Mexican American woman whose leg had been amputated in a car accident, was suing the Anglo driver who had caused the accident. Tijerina knew he had an airtight case—sure to bring her a substantial settlement—but only if he had a jury who could look past the race of the defendant and the plaintiff.

"I went and complained to Judge Roberts and he told me, he said, 'You know I don't discriminate, I'm fair,'" Tijerina recalled. The case was reset for August 1, 1966.

The second jury pool included two Spanish-surnamed jurors—one had been dead for ten years and the other spoke no English.

"As a result I was forced to settle for one-third the value of what it was actually worth," Tijerina said. "I was very upset."[3]

Yet that personal frustration was also Tijerina's epiphany: it was clear that extraordinary measures were needed to dismantle the racism rampant in Texas. The issue of jury selection was only one among many problems besetting Mexican Americans. They faced other forms of racism: police brutality, discrimination in housing, and employment and educational segregation to name just a few. Tijerina, practicing law in San Antonio, and other Mexican American attorneys, as well as other civil rights activists, recognized the impact of juries that could not identify with Spanish-speaking, usually low-income, defendants. "The [non-Latino] jurors were not the peers of my clients, who were poor people from the West Side," Tijerina said, referring to San Antonio, where his law office was located. "They [white jurors] wouldn't hesitate to render guilty verdicts."[4]

That 1966 courtroom disappointment compelled Tijerina to embark on the long, arduous process of creating an organization that could engage in the lengthy litigation required to finally do more than fight rampant discrimination piecemeal.

Tijerina didn't need to convince his fellow Mexican American lawyers of the need. One leading attorney, James DeAnda of Corpus Christi, laid out the issue of jury discrimination neatly in testimony to cabinet hearings in 1967. DeAnda traced how jury discrimination affected all facets of Latinos' lives:

[T]heir civil rights, their economic rights are affected just as are their personal privileges and liberty. Insurance companies are aware of this and there is a reluctance on the part of many insurance companies to issue liability insurance to minority groups simply because they think that a member of a minority group, when he goes to the courthouse, has two strikes against him; first, law enforcement prejudice, and second, juror and judicial prejudice. "An injured or dead Mexican isn't worth as much as an injured or dead Anglo" — I have had insurance company adjusters and lawyers blatantly make this statement to me in settlement negotiations and I have recognized the accuracy of what they say. Only a year ago one of my associates participated in a trial that resulted in a hung jury because one of the jurors believed and stated her position "that no Mexican was worth ten thousand dollars."[5]

The few Mexican Americans practicing law had profiles similar to Tijerina's and DeAnda's: most were the sons of working-class parents, had served in the military during World War II, and had used the G.I. Bill to go to college and then law school, expecting to change their world. But when they opened the doors of their practices, they found themselves at a decided disadvantage: the need for representation was great, the resources puny. Their low-income Mexican Americans clients appealed to them for relief. But too often the people couldn't afford attorney fees, were fearful of retribution, or were woefully ignorant of their rights.

Tijerina had seen it all since beginning his law practice in San Antonio in January 1952. At the time, he was thirty years old, ambitious and tough—willing to work hard to make a living for his wife and family and dedicated to bringing a better way of life for his clients. The racism prevalent throughout Texas was obvious to him: as the civil rights officer for the League of United Latin American Citizens (LULAC), Council 2, in San Antonio, Tijerina was inundated with complaints. His position at LULAC would put him at the forefront of Mexican American civil rights activism in Texas, if not the country. And it would soon lead to his selection as the key person to begin to assemble the group that would become the legal arm of the Mexican American civil rights movement.

This chapter examines the creation of MALDEF—the Mexican American Legal Defense and Educational Fund—and its first two years of operation until it was compelled to make major structural changes and relocate its headquarters from San Antonio to San Francisco. It offers a view into the creation of an important civil rights organization whose history is relatively unknown, even among students of Mexican American history. Yet MALDEF has grown into an organization that has taken the lead in almost all the national major litigation involving Mexican Americans, and more recently, Latinos. MALDEF's history links the World War II era of Mexican Americans to the Chicano movement a generation later, as well as to issues and personalities involved in Mexican American civil rights of the 1960s and 1970s. MALDEF's turmoil in its first two years was emblematic of the larger shifts among the greater Mexican American community—a tug of war between those who had worked through "the system" to achieve progress and others who were unsatisfied with the speed and extent of that progress.

In some ways, MALDEF's early difficulties and controversies may be partly attributed to a generational distrust that overlaid the civil rights movements in the 1960s—among African Americans, Latinos, and others.[6] But MALDEF's early adversities were exacerbated by longtime and deep-seated personal antagonisms and a struggle for power within a community that for too long had been denied self-determination. Finally, it is possible that the demands made on the founders and the goals they set for themselves in the early years were simply unrealistic and unfair. Perhaps all these problems were unavoidable given the explosive surge of activity that characterized MALDEF's first years.

The need for an organization such as MALDEF was undeniable. The larger Mexican American community had for many years struggled under discrimination and had fought back, individually and collectively, through organizations such as the League of United Latin American Citizens (LULAC) and the American G.I. Forum. Dozens of other groups had been short-lived.[7] There had been some postwar improvement, but progress was incremental. In the mid-1960s, the problems of Mexican Americans could no longer escape the notice of the largest of the philanthropies dedicated to social justice: the Ford Foundation.

BULWARKS AGAINST REPRESSION

MALDEF was not the first organization Mexican Americans had fashioned to resist repression. But MALDEF had key advantages over previous efforts in that at its inception there was both a critical mass of lawyers to press the cause and the philanthropic funding necessary to support it.[8] The Mexican American community was caught up in the upheaval sweeping across the United States; civil rights proponents encountered a chasm between conservative forces within the community and the grassroots activist elements. Conservatives exhorted changing the system from within—slowly—and in a way that would not alienate the white majority. Calling themselves "Chicanos," the more impatient activists, many of them in their early twenties, believed in a faster and more confrontational approach. One strategy was to empower the majority poor community and force change through external pressure.[9] It could be said that the World War II generation was made up of strivers—exceptional individuals who had dared to challenge enormous odds to force improvements for themselves and the Mexican American community. Their children had benefited from those changes. But when those younger people surveyed the status of Mexican Americans, they found pervasive inequalities: many of their group had been left behind. This Chicano generation concluded that there were structural reasons for the disparities: a system that privileged the dominant white society and relegated people of color to poverty and dehumanizing conditions. They set about creating their own activist organizations and fomenting protest—wishing to bring the dream of a fairer world to the general population, rather than to an elite few who had "made it." They staged protests, marches, and school walkouts, at which they held up placards and chanted slogans, and they sometimes got arrested for their actions.

It wasn't only the younger generation who had reached the conclusion that structural changes were necessary. There were some older Mexican Americans who were willing to support the newer activists—although not always through picket lines. Tijerina was one of the old guard who approved of the efforts of Chicano youth. In one newspaper article, he lauded them for their fearlessness: "My dilemma is that as a person, I'm a coward and do not march. I think of my family and myself first. . . . The Mexicano of the 1970s will have to take a stand or forever hide under the bed."[10]

There were only a few other Mexican American leaders of his generation willing to march and protest publicly. One of those was Bexar County commissioner Albert Peña Jr., an outspoken and blistering critic of the pervasive inequalities. He was one of the two best-known Mexican Americans in elected office in San Antonio in the late 1960s. The other was Congressman Henry B. Gonzalez.[11] Early on, the two men had been allies; Peña had worked for the Bexar County Democratic Party, in support of Gonzalez's successful congressional race in 1961. In 1960, Gonzalez, as national cochair of the Viva Kennedy campaign, had named Peña the Texas director.[12] But by 1969, the two men publicly clashed in the local San Antonio newspapers, which reported frequently on the enmity between the two prominent Mexican American leaders but were less inclined to analyze and determine the veracity of their charges and countercharges.

Into that world of longtime antagonisms and erupting frictions arrived Pete Tijerina and a small circle of Mexican American lawyers with a plan to build a new advocacy organization. As the main organizer, Tijerina would come in contact with a Who's Who of the Chicano/Mexican American civil rights movement, inspiring in them the hope of a more just legal system, persuading divergent groups to abandon their individual goals for a greater good, and on occasion becoming entangled in disputes that would hinder his best efforts.

From its beginning, MALDEF was pressed from all sides. Its members would navigate the many obstacles and issues, trying to determine their options, seeing how far they could push for greater equality, and calculating the cost of pushing those boundaries. MALDEF was not as independent as its leaders might have anticipated: its sole support in the early years was the Ford Foundation, which could and did make nuanced

FIGURE 3.1. *Pete Tijerina. Courtesy of the Voces Oral History Project.*

demands and which, finally, set hard conditions. Ford was itself under pressure: it operated under the vigilant eye of congressional leaders and journalists, and it worried about public perception, tax laws, and its own stewardship of its grants. Early on, after MALDEF became the focus of un-flattering news stories and the target of attacks on how it was spending Ford's money, the foundation tightened its hold on what appeared to be a promising program about to derail.

TIJERINA

Born in 1922 in Laredo, Texas, the son of a furniture mover and a housewife, Pedro "Pete" Tijerina didn't see many possibilities for himself growing up—and it is unlikely that others could envision him taking an important national leadership role. Two of the young Tijerina's positive character traits would come to serve him well in this capacity: a steely self-discipline that helped him shut out the world to concentrate on a task at hand and a resourcefulness that led him to find ways around formidable barriers, even when that meant challenging authority. These qualities would be honed over the years and set him on the path to establish MALDEF.

Tijerina was shaped by his hometown in many ways. Laredo was an anomaly for Mexican Americans: it was home to a host of middle- and upper-class Mexican American families, like the civic-minded Idars, who published a progressive newspaper and who sent their children to universities even before World War II. In Laredo, with its overwhelmingly Mexican American population, there were Mexican American professionals—teachers, doctors, bank presidents—unlike what could be seen in other Texas cities.[13] Tijerina pounced on the few opportunities that presented themselves. But his horizons were limited; a high school education seemed unnecessary. He dropped out of Martin High School in the ninth grade and went to work for New Deal programs: first the Citizens Military Training Corps (CMTC), designed for young men, and then the Civilian Conservation Corps.[14] At the Citizens Military Training Corps, Tijerina got a taste of discrimination when the Mexican American teenagers—and not the Anglos—were ordered to report for crew cuts. The seventy-five Mexican Americans at the camp elected Tijerina as their representative to protest the order, an acknowledgement of the regard his classmates held for his leadership. Tijerina argued their cause and was booted out of the corps for his outspokenness. It would be his first brush with civil rights advocacy.[15]

In August 1941, Tijerina joined the U.S. Air Force and was assigned to work as a guard at Brooks Air Force Base in San Antonio, and later as an aircraft propeller mechanic. In 1945, in the waning weeks of the war, he was sent to Guam, where he made friends with other Latinos, united, he would say later, by the Spanish language. Throughout his time in the service, the high school dropout read voraciously—initially for pleasure. But soon the reading took on a new purpose: mapping his future. Irving Stone's biography of Clarence Darrow touched him deeply.[16] "That guided me towards law," Tijerina said. "The book was about Clarence Darrow fighting for the oppressed and the poor and I thought, 'Maybe this is where I belong.'"

Tijerina returned to Texas after the war, interested in law school. One minor problem: he had no high school diploma. Undeterred, Tijerina sought out his high school principal to see if something might be done— short of reentering high school.

"My principal, J. W. Nixon, told me, 'Pete, if you pass the college entrance exam to [the University of] Texas, I'll give you your diploma,'" Tijerina recalled. Tijerina passed the exam (he attributed his success to his heavy reading in the service) and got his high school diploma. He attended UT–Austin from 1946 to 1948, where he became involved with LULAC and afterward started law school at St. Mary's University in San Antonio. But Tijerina's low grades forced him into a grueling schedule. To improve his grades, he also enrolled in the South Texas College of Law in Houston, about two hundred miles away. Twice a week and on Saturdays, he took night classes in Houston and on two other weekday nights he took classes at St. Mary's. At the same time, he was working full-time for the Department of Public Safety.

In the end, St. Mary's refused to accept his grades from the Houston law school and suspended him for scholastic reasons. Tijerina had one last chance—and it was a long shot: he would be allowed to take his bar exam without finishing law school *if* a practicing lawyer sponsored him and let him complete his studies under the lawyer's supervision, a practice known as "reading for the bar." Tijerina rose to the challenge, securing the cooperation of municipal judge Jimmy Tafolla, and locking himself up in a room at the Robert E. Lee Hotel in downtown San Antonio, where he studied nonstop for thirty days. The only time he left the room, he recalled, was to grab a bite at the coffee shop downstairs.

Tijerina passed the bar in 1951 and began to practice in January 1952. He became a criminal trial lawyer, "learning by trial and error," he said, and taking whatever cases he could get.

He also joined a local LULAC chapter, Council 2, an organization in which he had been active at the University of Texas. As an attorney, his work with LULAC Council 2 revolved around civil rights issues, hearing complaints from Mexican Americans with a host of problems: police brutality, abuse of authority, lack of access to public accommodation, unfair employment practices, and segregated schools. He became LULAC's state civil rights chair, not much more than a title as his portfolio came with scant resources. But here he built a network of like-minded people, in-

FIGURE 3.2. *Jack Greenberg. Courtesy of the Voces Oral History Project.*

cluding lawyers in other cities and journalists sympathetic to the cause of racial justice. But actually effecting change was another matter. Tijerina's only recourse involved passing resolutions; filing petitions; and sending sternly worded letters to school boards, city councils, and police departments, hoping for change. The resolutions had little effect; they could easily be tossed into a wastebasket. Tijerina could only shine a spotlight on the problem: news about the LULAC complaints were carried by sympathetic newspapers. "The press was very good to me," Tijerina recalled. "I was making a name for myself." [17] Later, he would hear that some of those news clippings about Tijerina's work made their way to the New York offices of the NAACP Legal Defense and Educational Fund, where they were read with growing interest by the NAACP's lead counsel, Jack Greenberg.

JACK GREENBERG

While Pete Tijerina was building fences for the CCC (Civilian Conservation Corps) in South Texas, one of his contemporaries, Jack Greenberg, two years younger than Tijerina, was attending high school at DeWitt Clinton, in the Bronx (New York). Greenberg had advantages in New York that Tijerina couldn't enjoy. Living in the city exposed the Greenberg family to some of the great institutions, such as Columbia University. Greenberg's mother, a Romanian immigrant who herself had little formal education, opened a savings account for Jack's college education when he was a baby, depositing fifty cents every week "for [his] tuition to go to Columbia, the only school she ever considered." [18] Greenberg expected to become an accountant like his father, a Polish immigrant, as well as a lawyer.[19] He attributed his own outlook on life to his father's disregard of authority, a determination to decide for himself after studying a matter; "he didn't endorse the status quo."[20] As his mother had envisioned, Greenberg was accepted and attended Columbia University, but his studies were interrupted at the end of his junior year in 1944 when he was called to active duty in the U.S. Navy and sent to Cornell University as part of its V-12 officer-training program.[21] Greenberg later served on a landing-ship tank (LST 715) as a deck officer and participated in the invasion of Iwo Jima, later traveling to Saipan, Okinawa, and Iheya Shima.

Like Tijerina, Greenberg demonstrated a commitment to righting wrongs. His moment came while he was at sea in the navy.

> Once I did approach the line the other side of which was court-martial: The captain confined a sailor to the brig, which on this ship was the locker where the anchor chain was stored, on bread and water, without a trial, for some trivial wrongdoing. The captain wouldn't release the prisoner nor would he give him a trial. I went to the captain's cabin and asked that he release the man. We had a shouting match. He threatened me with a court-martial; I said I would inform his superior. I was so tense that when I left his cabin I cried. To my surprise the captain backed down and released the sailor.[22]

While Greenberg was in the Pacific, he was granted his degree in absentia from Columbia in 1945. After his discharge from the navy, Greenberg began Columbia Law School in the fall of 1946 and graduated in October 1948.[23] Greenberg took four semesters of a half-credit "legal survey" class under Professor Walter Gellhorn, in which he and his classmates provided legal assistance to groups on matters of civil liberties and civil rights. One group he worked with was the NAACP Legal Defense and Educational Fund, or the LDF, which was founded in 1948 and whose board overlapped with, but was legally separate from, the NAACP.[24]

When the LDF was looking for a lawyer, Gellhorn recommended Greenberg and Thurgood Marshall, the LDF's special counsel, hired him. Greenberg's new job as staff attorney put him in the thick of the civil rights movement, seeing firsthand the discrimination against African Americans in the South, and earned him Marshall's confidence. The case that would prove pivotal for the LDF, for Marshall, and for Greenberg was the historic *Oliver Brown, et al. v. Board of Education of Topeka, et al.* (commonly

FIGURE 3.3. *Standing, left to right: John J. Herrera, Houston; Albert Peña, Jr., San Antonio; Al Hernandez, Houston; Frank M. Pinedo, Austin; Carlos C. Cadena, San Antonio; David Longoria, Austin; Leo Duran, Corpus Christi; Gus C. Garcia, San Diego, Texas; and William Bonilla, Corpus Christi. Seated, left to right: Hector De Peña, Corpus Christi; and Homero Lopez, Kingsville, 1954. Courtesy of Special Collections and Archives, Bell Library, Texas A&M University, Corpus Christi.*

cited as *Brown v. Board of Education*), which outlawed school segregation, determining that separate facilities were inherently unequal.[25] The victory raised the profiles of LDF's work and of Marshall's legal skills. Marshall was appointed to the U.S. Court of Appeals in 1961, and as he prepared to leave he recommended that Greenberg take his place as director-counsel of the LDF.[26]

But even while representing African American concerns, the LDF was also moved by the plight of other minorities. By the mid-1960s, Greenberg was receiving requests for assistance from Mexican Americans and Native Americans. Greenberg knew the need far exceeded the LDF's capacity.[27] To handle those cases, the LDF created the National Office for the Rights of the Indigent and reached out to Tijerina to help litigate Mexican American cases.

OUR OWN LAWYERS

In early 1967, Tijerina wrote to the University of Texas education professor George I. Sanchez, asking for Sanchez's thoughts on the possibility of working with the LDF. Sanchez had long supported pursuing legal remedies, raising money for the Hernandez case in 1954 through the American Council of Spanish-speaking People and finding funds to fight discrimination in public housing in California, Texas, and Arizona.[28] Now Tijerina told Sanchez that he had been corresponding with the LDF about the possibility of taking a test case involving Mexican American jury representation. Tijerina recommended six attorneys from around the state, including himself. And he added: "Jimmy DeAnda from Corpus Christi . . . came up with the suggestion that if the lawyers named herein work as a group we could try to get direct funding from the Ford Foundation instead of having to rely on the Legal Defense Fund."[29]

Sanchez wrote back promptly, saying he was "lukewarm" about joining forces with the LDF because, he said, discrimination against blacks was based on race, while discrimination against Mexican Americans was based on reasons that "are much more varied and very different." He concluded, "[R]iding the coat tails of the NAACP is bad strategy. Cooperation, yes. Why can't we push for a Mexican-American Legal Defense Fund of our own? The last paragraph states that Jimmy DeAnda thinks this way also. Count me in."[30]

Tijerina had, in fact, already worked with the LDF on a grand jury discrimination case, after his work with LULAC Council 2 came to the attention of Jack Greenberg.[31] Afterward, Greenberg invited Tijerina to a civil rights lawyers' conference in Chicago, offering to cover his expenses. Initially, Tijerina was unreceptive to Greenberg's overture to attend the conference, but after he was forced to settle for a lesser amount in the amputee civil lawsuit in Jourdanton, he was ready to see what Greenberg had in mind.

Tijerina was unable to travel to Chicago for the meeting, but he arranged for attorney Matt Garcia to take his place.[32] Garcia reported back that the LDF had "money, plenty of money."[33]

Armed with Garcia's report, Tijerina telephoned Greenberg, who initially suggested that a new LDF affiliate, the National Office for the Rights of the Indigent (NORI), come to San Antonio to take the cases. But Tijerina pushed for an organization independent of NORI and the LDF. "It was important to the movement, and to the cause, and to the Mexican American community that we have our own lawyers fight our own cases," he said.[34]

Tijerina's use of the phrases "the movement" and "the cause" are telling. His brand of advocacy was linked to the nascent Chicano movement. But his approach would also see MALDEF collide with the more conservative element of the Mexican American community.

For Greenberg, helping launch a Mexican American civil rights counterpart to the NAACP Legal Defense and Educational Fund was consistent with his work relating to other groups. He was willing to use his own contacts and wherewithal to help his Mexican American colleagues, as he would also try to help Native Americans, Puerto Ricans, and later gays and lesbians.[35] As for women, Greenberg led efforts in New York City to do away with a common practice in private clubs to exclude women. After several setbacks, a city ordinance was passed in 1984 to outlaw the practice.

Greenberg recounted the telephone conversation with Tijerina: "I outlined what they would have to do," Greenberg said. "I would have to get money from foundations and would have to give a credible report on why they needed the money and what they would do with it." [36]

Ten days after that initial phone call, Greenberg called Tijerina back: he had scheduled a meeting in New York with representatives of the Ford Foundation and he would send Tijerina five hundred dollars to travel to New York. Tijerina brought with him two other lawyers: Roy Padilla, who served on the San Antonio City Council from 1961 to 1965 as part of a slate presented by the conservative Good Government League; and Bexar County commissioner Albert Peña, a "militant civil rights leader." [37] Padilla's daughter was an airline flight attendant, so Padilla flew for free. Tijerina gave his five hundred dollars to Peña and paid his own way. With the participation of Padilla and Peña, Tijerina covered the political spectrum from conservative to the Far Left.[38]

For two hours, seven men sat at La Fonda del Sol, a restaurant in midtown Manhattan—Tijerina, Peña, and Padilla explaining the plight of Mexican Americans in Texas to Greenberg, the Ford Foundation's legal programs officer William Pincus, and two other Ford staffers.[39] "School segregation, non-participation in juries, employment discrimination— we talked about everything," Tijerina said. At the conclusion of the lunch meeting, the Ford officers estimated that to build a detailed proposal that would meet the foundation's requirements, it would cost around six thousand dollars.

"I says, 'We don't have it,'" Tijerina recalled. "Jack Greenberg says, 'Wait a minute.' He went out to a pay phone and called a friend of his. . . . In ten minutes he was back and he says, 'You've got your $6,000,'" Tijerina said.[40] "'Now we're gonna talk about who's going to write your proposal.'"[41]

Tijerina proposed two possible grant writers: Joe Bernal, a state senator, or José A. Cárdenas, superintendent of the Edgewood schools in San Antonio. But Greenberg countered with another recommendation: Mike Finkelstein, whose statistical analysis and research had provided the demographic analyses for *Brown v. Board of Education*. Tijerina said he had no quarrel with having Finkelstein work on the proposal.

About a week later, the Ford Foundation called Tijerina with a more expansive idea. "[Ford officials said,] 'We think we would be interested in funding a civil rights organization for the Mexican Americans covering the entire Southwest,'" Tijerina recalled. "'So you can amend whatever papers you are going to prepare.'"

The second issue the foundation wanted to discuss was that of competing proposals. "'If there is a competing proposal, we'll cancel you out, close the book,'" Tijerina recalled the foundation officials telling him.

Tijerina put aside all else and plunged into setting up the legal framework for the new organization, building support across the Southwest, neutralizing any possible competitors, and working with Finkelstein on a grant proposal. Thus began a new phase for Pete Tijerina: that of organizer. "I had no idea of the problems in the other states," Tijerina admitted later.[42] He would find like-minded people throughout the Southwest. He would also become aware of how widespread and entrenched was the discrimination against Mexican Americans. Building support would prove easy compared to the larger challenge he would find later in administering a major grant and fending off powerful critics.

BUILDING A CIVIL RIGHTS ORGANIZATION

Why build a new organization rather than attach one to an existing group or groups, such as the League of United Latin American Citizens or the American G.I. Forum? Tijerina was already a member of both. And, if the Mexican American civil rights group was to be modeled after the NAACP Legal Defense and Educational Fund, it might have seemed appropriate to create it out of LULAC.

But there were reasons for eschewing such alignments, and they were political as well as historical. The G.I. Forum's focus was narrower than what Greenberg and Tijerina envisioned: the forum had been created specifically to handle veterans' rights, although it was also involved in general Mexican American civil rights causes; education was a key issue. But the forum was closely identified with its founder, the Corpus Christi physician Hector P. Garcia. And although Garcia enjoyed the respect of Mexican Americans, this new organization might be perceived as being another organization of Garcia's rather than a new one. It was important that this fledgling organization be independent of existing organizations.

LULAC could also offer an infrastructure of supporters. The oldest—it was established in Corpus Christi in 1929—and largest Mexican American organization, LULAC had chapters, or councils, throughout the country. Tijerina was well respected for his work as LULAC's Texas civil rights leader. But the organization was not universally respected. Carlos Cadena, an esteemed San Antonio attorney who was on the first board of MALDEF and would serve as its first president, was dismissive of LULAC, suggesting that the organization was used by some as merely a networking tool rather than as a way to fight discrimination.

"They [LULAC] had businessmen that didn't want to make you [opponents of Mexican American civil rights efforts] mad, because you wouldn't buy a piano from them—or something like that," Cadena said. "But Hector [Garcia of the American G.I. Forum] and his group were ACTIVISTS." [43]

Perhaps the more fundamental reason for creating a new organization was the precedent set by the NAACP and LDF. Greenberg and others could attest to the minefields that might await MALDEF if it was tied to an existing organization. The NAACP and the NAACP Legal Defense Fund were far apart. Since giving permission to the Legal Defense Fund to use its name in 1938, the NAACP had periodically sought to reverse that decision. The NAACP charged that its and the LDF's fund-raising outreach too often overlapped, with each vying for support from the same sources. The NAACP also complained that the LDF represented competitors of the NAACP, such as Martin Luther King Jr., the Congress of Racial Equality (CORE), and the Student Nonviolent Coordinating Committee (SNCC). The NAACP also complained that many couldn't tell the two organizations apart.[44] The friction eventually culminated in a 1978 lawsuit brought by the NAACP against the LDF, calling for the LDF to drop NAACP from its name. Seven years later, a federal court of appeals dismissed the suit, concluding that the claim was a "stale one" and that the NAACP had not demonstrated that it had attempted to negotiate its differences with the LDF.[45]

In the end, there was no serious consideration of building from an existing organization. MALDEF was incorporated on May 24, 1967, with the Texas secretary of state. Signers were Tijerina, Albert A. Peña Jr., and Roy Padilla. It would become clear later that even a new organization will bear the history, political entanglements, and hostilities of its organizers and board members. One observer was the Texas congressman Henry B. Gonzalez, who shared an intense and mutual animosity with Albert A. Peña Jr. Gonzalez would come to have a tremendous influence over MALDEF.

But at the time of its incorporation, Tijerina knew only that there was a new organization to be formed and collaborators to recruit. With his wife, Graciela Gonzalez Tijerina, at the wheel of the family car, Tijerina visited major Mexican American population centers throughout the Southwest, relying on an informal network of lawyer friends and LULAC members to meet local Mexican American attorneys and present his case.

The few Mexican American attorneys practicing were well known in their respective communities—many were active in organizations such as LULAC. In El Paso, Albert Armendariz, who had been the LULAC president in 1953, had at one time worked closely with Tijerina. In fact, their close collaboration had nearly gotten both of them impeached from their LULAC offices—Armendariz as national president and Tijerina as the LULAC Council 2 scholarship chairman—for misappropriation of funds. They openly admitted they had taken the funds. But, they said, there were good reasons: at the time, the Hernandez jury case was heading to the Supreme Court and the lawyers handling the case needed two thousand dollars for court fees. Tijerina and Armendariz knew this jury discrimination case was key in the civil rights struggle; there was, in their minds, no activity more important at that time. Neither man had the necessary sum at their personal disposal, but they did have LULAC scholarship funds. Without securing proper authorization, they simply withdrew money from the scholarship accounts to pay court fees.

Years later, Armendariz would marvel at what he considered misplaced priorities of his fellow LULACers: "I took $1,000 out of my [LULAC national scholarship] account, Pete took $1,000 out of his [local scholarship] account, we gave it to them and *Hernandez vs. Texas* went to the

Supreme Court. . . . Both of us faced impeachment by the LULACs. Both of us were maligned by the LULACs for taking funds . . . because they didn't understand that there are things more important than scholarships."[46]

The episode reinforced the importance of having an organization that would be charged with *and* have sufficient resources available for costly and lengthy litigation.

In New Mexico, Tijerina asked for the intercession of a former colleague, Manuel Lopez, who had moved there and was now working for a federally funded program, SER-Jobs for Progress.

"As I was addressing the problems of Mexican Americans here and there and everywhere, somebody raised his hand and said, 'Mr. Tijerina, we're not Mexican Americans in New Mexico; we're Spanish Americans,'" Tijerina recalled with a smile.

"I said, 'Well, look, for the time being, just go along with me. Wait 'til we get the money and then you can call yourself whatever you want,'" Tijerina said.[47] The Hispano lawyers agreed. Dan Sosa, a former assistant U.S. attorney, was recruited to be the New Mexico representative to MALDEF.

In Los Angeles, Herman Sillas gave local support.[48] But Tijerina learned that Bert Corona, a well-respected Los Angeles–based union organizer and activist, was developing a Ford Foundation proposal to provide legal assistance to Mexican Americans. Tijerina and Corona met at ten one night and talked until five the following morning.

"Finally we gave each other the *abrazo* [embrace] and he agreed to yield to the San Antonio group," Tijerina said.

Later Tijerina learned that some California lawyers "didn't want any damned Mexicanos from Texas telling Mexicanos from California what to do."[49]

Tijerina also met with the United Farm Workers' Cesar Chavez, who already had connections at Ford. Tijerina first assured Chavez that MALDEF would work with the UFW, and that MALDEF's and the UFW's fundraising efforts would not compete.[50]

Tijerina was meanwhile building a board of directors. The only non–Mexican American was Jack Greenberg; the only nonlawyer was state senator Joe Bernal.[51] The bylaws were approved unanimously nine months later in the Bluebonnet Room of the Gunter Hotel in San Antonio. Carlos Cadena was named president, Tijerina was named executive director.[52]

FIGURE 3.4. *George I. Sanchez. Courtesy of the Nettie Lee Benson Latin American Collection, General Libraries, University of Texas at Austin.*

THE FORD FOUNDATION

In 1975, seven years after MALDEF's incorporation, Bernal assented to a request from MALDEF board chairman Richard A. Ibañez of Los Angeles to spearhead a Texas Amigos de MALDEF and "to effect as big a financial return as possible from Texas." In his letter to Ibañez, Bernal mused about what a difference foundation funding had made.

> I remember the late Dr. George I. Sanchez proudly saying that back in the good 'ole days they had to nickel and dime the support of such cases as the *Hernandez* jury discrimination case and that people really felt it was *their* case. However proud we could all be of the great effort of our forebears at a time when they didn't have the Ford or other foundation *chiches* [teats] — the fact still remains that we would still be crawling towards that seemingly illusory goal of access to full and complete freedom under this great democracy. The effort to gain our civil rights has surely been sped up because of Ford and other Foundations assisting us.[53]

Bernal's blunt assessment of the critical importance of outside financial support was inarguable. The Mexican American community for decades had organized against discrimination — dating back to the mutual-aid societies of the 1880s.[54] But only a few of those earlier Mexican American organizations were dedicated to working through the judicial system — and none could be sustained for long: the problems were too pervasive, the need too great. And there were too few lawyers trained and economically secure enough to take on the lengthy litigation needed to overcome institutionalized racism.

But in the 1960s, the Ford Foundation, the largest at that time both in terms of assets and annual giving, turned its gaze and opened its checkbook to the Mexican American community.

Founded in 1936 in Dearborn, Michigan, with 90 percent of the stock of the Ford Motor Company, the Ford Foundation had become a leading philanthropic organization advocating for social justice. Had the Edsel Division of Ford Motor Company and Henry Ford given the stock to their heirs rather than establish a foundation, those heirs would have promptly faced enormous inheritance taxes. The foundation instead used the stocks' dividends for philanthropic purposes.[55] Early Ford grants were made mostly to Michigan institutions until the foundation moved to New York in 1953.[56] Over the years the Ford Foundation met with criticism, alternately accused of being too left leaning and, at other times, too "establishment." [57] In the early 1950s, for instance, it was accused, in news stories published in the *Chicago Tribune*, of showing a "leftist slant." Journalist Dwight Macdonald, writing about the foundation, noted that ultraconservative columnist Westbrook Pegler called the Ford Foundation "'a front for dangerous Communists,' while *Pravda* rather inclines to the view that 'the real business of the Ford foundation is the sending of spies, murderers, saboteurs, and wreckers to Eastern Europe.'" [58]

The foundation came under congressional scrutiny at various times. Two congressional probes between 1952 and 1956, Macdonald wrote, were "instituted on the ostensible ground that the republic was or might possibly be or maybe had been or perhaps was going to be in danger from the foundations. In reality, both were merely episodes in Republican factional politics." [59] But other investigations, including the 1969 probe launched by Congressman Wright Patman (D-TX), resulted in major changes to the tax laws related to charitable foundations. [60] The part of the new tax code that would emerge as a problem for MALDEF and the Ford Foundation in 1970 would ban grants that would influence legislation or support political campaigns.

As early as 1964, the Ford Foundation had shown an interest in addressing the Mexican American community. Before making a major commitment to Mexican Americans, the East Coast–based nonprofit sought to understand the issues facing the Southwest-centered people. But the attempt met with criticism by Chicano academics who viewed the effort as ham-fisted, perhaps a foreshadowing of the turbulence that lay ahead. In 1964, Ford's director of public affairs programs, Paul Ylvisaker, commissioned a five-year study, headed by the UCLA professor Leo Grebler, on the status of Mexican Americans. [61] The second author was Joan Moore, who had moved to California from Chicago in the early 1960s and acknowledged in 1997 that before she arrived in Los Angeles, she had never been exposed to Mexican Americans. [62] The study included as third author Ralph C. Guzmán, a political scientist and historian, who was also a Mexican-born former migrant farmworker and a World War II merchant mariner and navy veteran. [63] Vocal Chicano academics denounced the Grebler study for what they characterized as a patronizing and naive tone. The critiques raised important questions about the role of scholars, "objectivity" in research, and the lagging numbers of Chicano academics who could have been recruited to conduct the work. *Social Science Quarterly*, the journal of the largest organization of sociologists, published five review articles in its June 1971 issue. All reviewers recognized the Grebler book's "landmark" status—it was the first time that Mexican Americans had been studied in such detail. Because it was the first of its kind, it was credited as foundational to future research. The sociologist Norval Glenn noted that the study signified "the new importance of Chicanos in the eyes of foundations, educational agencies, and academicians."[64] Still, he said, it was expected that many Chicano academics would resent that it was written by Anglo scholars.[65]

The UC–Santa Barbara professor Jesús Chavarría especially chafed at Grebler's assertion that "when our research got under way, the definition of Mexican Americans as a national minority was almost as novel to the larger society as it was to the minority itself." Chavarría wrote that Chicanos in the study were never portrayed as "protagonists. That part is reserved for the author."[66] Chavarría condemned what he called the study's "indifference to Mexican Americans as a living people."[67] By the time the research began, Chavarría said, there were already protest actions taking place: student organizations in the Bay Area of Northern California; Cesar Chavez's farmworker grape strikes, Reies Lopez Tijerina's Alianza in New Mexico, a Chicano youth movement. Grebler et al. had chosen to characterize those efforts as "fringe problems" and, for the youth protests, "paralleling the new black consciousness . . . [i]nstead of listening to the Chicano's own voice our author stuck to his purpose; he would make the nation aware, in his own fashion, of the Mexican Americans as 'the nation's second largest minority.'"[68]

Ylvisaker of Ford was not relying solely on the Grebler book. He also appointed three respected activists, organizers, and academics as national affairs consultants: Herman Gallegos, an organizer with the Community Service Organization (cso); Ernesto Galarza, a labor economist and champion of farmworker rights; and the Notre Dame sociologist Julian Samora. Their charge was to explore possible philanthropic support and to recommend solutions for the problems facing the Mexican American community. That attention prompted other foundations to consider Mexican American causes.[69]

Meanwhile, there were unrelated efforts that would come to directly impact Ford's Mexican American interests. The LDF had begun receiving some Ford funding for its NORI arm and had established good relations with the foundation's staff.[70] The fund, through NORI, had also taken on a few cases related to Native Americans and Mexican Americans. By 1968, NORI had ten cases focusing on Mexican Americans and six on Native Americans.[71] Greenberg recognized the need for a more targeted effort related to both groups. Pete Tijerina in San Antonio was making news there as the civil rights officer of LULAC's Council 2, drawing attention to rampant discrimination against Mexican Americans.

Ford officials floated the concept of a Mexican American legal defense organization, with the LDF taking the lead, to the labor economist Ernesto Galarza.[72] But Galarza was skeptical. In a September 1967 letter to S. M. Miller, who took over from Ylvisaker as director of public affairs programs after 1966, Galarza lauded the foundation for its willingness to take on the creation of the organization. The problems facing Mexican Americans were "serious and widespread . . . the gap between injuries and legal remedies in the field of civil rights is unquestionably widened by the absence of a cadre of Mexican-American lawyers trained and experienced in this field."

But while such an organization might be "technically effective," Galarza cautioned, it may miss the more substantial problem, particularly if it was modeled after the LDF:

> The Legal Defense and Educational Fund was, I think, an outgrowth of the organizational base of the NAACP in the Negro community. There is no such base in the Mexican American community presently.
>
> I have no doubt that with the help of [the] NAACP the available and interested Mexican-American attorneys could put together a technically effective program.
>
> But I am of the opinion that the proposal looks too narrowly at such technical efficiency, well within reach of the persons already committed. In fact, the emphasis placed by the proposal on community education, the rights of public protest and assistance to the community (beyond assistance to individual) suggest a tentative awareness of the point I am raising.[73]

Galarza worried that the Mexican American civil rights organization would move far ahead of its base; the litigation demands on those attorneys' time would preclude them from educating the community about their rights.

"If I am not mistaken, then, I would suggest that the community education and action implications of the proposal be clearly defined," he wrote.

Admitting that his idea was vague, he nonetheless suggested the formation of a modestly funded local civil rights educational committee composed of grass-roots citizens and provided with the necessary technical assistance in community organization. Such a committee, through a well conceived program of educational and activist relationships upward to the legal skills and outward to the community, would, in my judgment, help to create in the long run the base I spoke of before.

Would it be desirable to make such a grant to the proposed Southwest council we have talked about, under express obligation to work out, with lawyers and community workers, a workable scheme of this type?[74]

Miller, in a September 1967 memo to William Pincus, the foundation's legal programs officer, five days later referred to the council idea: "As part of our plans, we propose to support a Council of the Southwest for Mexican-American Affairs. Ernie [Galarza] wants this council to play a major role in developing some legal programs; whether as a substitute for the Legal Defense proposal, I am not sure. Let us discuss?"[75]

But by the time that Galarza was registering his concerns, Tijerina had already written to Pincus, notifying him that the Ford proposal, coordinated and written by him and Finkelstein, would be arriving shortly. "I sincerely hope that our efforts will not be in vain," Tijerina said.

Tijerina said that following the meeting at La Fonda del Sol, he had visited and spoken to "most of the Mexican American Lawyers in California, New Mexico, Arizona, and Colorado," adding, "[T]hey are unanimous in expressing the need for this program and share our concern for the increasing unrest of the Mexican American labeled the poorest of the poor."

"Needless to say[,] the law practice has suffered[;] however, I am committed and will follow your instructions to the letter," he said.

Tijerina indicated he was aware of other Ford initiatives to support Mexican Americans. He offered: "[I]f I can provide a similar service in Texas, please do not hesitate to call on me and I will accept your assignment without any compensation."[76]

The Ford program officer responsible for the foundation's Hispanic project funding from 1968 to 1981, Siobhan O. Nicolau, writing with Henry Santiestevan, labor organizer and former head of the Southwest (later National) Council of La Raza, summed up the priorities of the large Latino nonprofits that emerged in the 1960s: "The early agenda required massive organization, the creation of stable institutions, and the preparation of a large cadre of leaders experienced and sophisticated in advocacy, fundraising, and institutional management. None of that could take place without resources—and resources were a scarce commodity." [77]

Why had it taken so long to start up an organization like MALDEF? Nicolau writes that there were several factors. Adequate funding was essential. Mexican Americans were generally inexperienced in mounting the types of programs most attractive to foundations; the foundations were reluctant to take a chance on untried projects. Corporate funders were not yet an option—until ethnic marketing became popular, they shied away from "ethnic organizations." And the federal government was determined to maintain good terms with the local and state officials, "many of whom were none too pleased with the rising tide of Mexican-Americans who wanted full societal participation. In addition, the liberal, professional whites who had played a significant role in supporting the black movement were in short supply in the Southwest." [78]

Nicolau and Santiestevan agreed with Galarza about a lack of infrastructure in the Mexican American community and offered other insights as well: "They [Mexican Americans] lacked the strong network of religious institutions that had nurtured black leadership, they lacked visibility outside the Southwest and they lacked a history of slavery, a powerful tool that had galvanized white guilt and support for the black civil rights movement." [79]

In the 1960s, Nicolau and Santiestevan wrote, social programs dedicated to helping minorities were geared to African Americans without tending to the needs of other groups, including Mexican Americans.[80]

Tijerina was learning quickly about the importance of keeping potential benefactors apprised of his efforts and needs. In a letter to the Ford Foundation's William Pincus, Tijerina wrote that he was involved with organizing a march of farmworkers from the Rio Grande Valley "from New Braunfels to the capitol in Austin, Texas, to again resubmit our petition for a state minimum wage law of $1.25 per hour, but believe me that it is very difficult to operate without funds." [81]

Pincus responded to Tijerina a week later that the foundation had received the proposal, assuring Tijerina that it would receive "every consideration." Then he asked a nagging question: *Are you sure about "Mexican American" in the name?*

"I realize that the term Mexican American is of a special reference in the west and southwest because of the history linking that part of the United States and Mexico," Pincus wrote. "My question really is would a term like this arouse any adverse reaction on the part of any other Spanish-Americans?" [82]

Tijerina responded in a letter five days later that the term "Mexican American" was one that had been adopted with the consent of the various state leaders. Tijerina said that over the previous ten days, he had met with "leaders and attorneys in Denver and Pueblo in the state of Colorado and Santa Fe, Albuquerque and Las Cruces in the state of New Mexico."

"The people from the state of New Mexico have always prefered [*sic*] to be identified as Spanish-Americans, however, they are 100 percent behind this program and in fact the person that is being considered as the director or chief counsel is Lawrence Tapia, a young attorney from Albuquerque, New Mexico."[83]

Throughout the period of exchanges with Ford and meetings with lawyers throughout the Southwest, Tijerina and a small group had been working on bylaws for the new group. On February 16, 1968, the group's bylaws were adopted. Pete Tijerina was named executive director, in recognition of his key role in establishing the organization. Carlos C. Cadena, known for his role as an attorney in the Hernandez case, was named president and presided over the meeting.[84]

THE GRANT PROPOSAL

The proposal written by Tijerina and Finkelstein noted that in 1967, the Ford Foundation had funded the National Office for the Rights of the Indigent (NORI) and had become aware of the problems of Mexican Americans in the Southwest. Funding for the proposal writing was funneled through NORI.

"It is NORI's conclusion, and the conclusion of Mexican-American leaders themselves, that civil rights problems of Mexican-Americans are serious and widespread and that various approaches to them are needed, including the creation of a separate organization to deal with them through action in the courts."[85]

The proposal outlined the need:

- The 1959 census found that over one-third of all Mexican American families—a figure double that of Anglos—lived below the poverty line of $3,000.
- Mexican American median educational attainment was 7.1 years compared to 9.0 for nonwhites and 12.1 for Anglos.
- The school dropout rate for Mexican American children was about 50 percent.

- Mexican American children attended segregated and inferior schools that emphasized vocational, rather than academic, preparation.
- Mexican Americans were not enrolling in colleges and universities in large numbers. As an example: at the University of California's Berkeley campus, with an enrollment of 26,083, there were only 231 Negroes and 76 Mexican Americans in the student body; at the UCLA campus, in an enrollment of 26,000, there were 70 Mexican Americans.
- Charges of police brutality were too numerous to catalog. "Deaths of Mexican American boys are reported in California, Colorado, and Texas . . . . In only a few instances have suits been brought against the police" (8).[86]
- Juries: "In Texas, the 'key man' system is used, that is, the jury commissioners ask persons well known in the community, almost invariably Anglos, to obtain names for the jury panel. This method results in only token numbers of Mexican-Americans being called for jury service. While there have been more than a dozen cases involving jury discrimination against Negroes to reach the United States Supreme Court, there has been only one such case involving Mexican-Americans" (9).
- An estimated half million Mexicans were in the United States illegally. "Fear of irregular status or the desire to avoid any action which would jeopardize the entry of relatives is said to chill civic activities on the part of Mexican-Americans" (11).
- "In Texas, the Registration Act of 1966 (enacted simultaneously with the repeal of the poll tax) limits time for registration to approximately four months during the winter and requires annual registration. Mexican-Americans believe this law was passed to replace the poll tax as a barrier to their registration" (12).
- Intimidation: In the 1964 general election in San Antonio, "Texas Rangers appeared at polling places in Mexican-American districts and used cameras, apparently taking pictures of the voters. They did not appear at Anglo polling stations" (12–13).
- Political representation: In Los Angeles, with 1 million Mexican Americans, there were no Mexican Americans on the city council, the state assembly, or state senate. One, Ed Roybal, was serving in Congress.

Because of a shortage of Mexican American lawyers, it was extremely difficult to bring the law to bear on these problems, in general. There was an even more serious dearth of lawyers trained and able to take on the lengthy litigation required in civil rights suits:

- Although the Mexican American population of the Southwest was 10 percent; only 2.1 percent of all attorneys were Mexican American. "In cities like Eagle Pass, [San] Angelo, Lubbock, Fort Worth, there was only one Mexican American lawyer in town" (15).
- Almost all Mexican American lawyers either were sole practitioners or were in "loose associations with other lawyers. . . . Their cases were mostly divorces, negligence, immigration and criminal cases and they had no steady retainers from big business corporations" (16). The Mexican American lawyers' incomes reflected the general poverty of Mexican Americans: in 1959, the median earnings of Mexican American lawyers in Texas was $7,405, while that of all lawyers in Texas was $9,734 (17).
- Mexican American lawyers were so busy just trying to make a living off the high volume, low-cost work that they could not afford to provide the pro bono effort to civil rights cases.
- The Mexican American community was too poor to pay "even modest counsel fees" for those cases (17).[87]
- Mexican American lawyers had virtually no experience in civil rights cases. "Most Mexican-American lawyers interviewed in the preparation of this proposal had neither handled a case in federal court . . . [nor] litigated a federal constitutional claim.
- "*Not one lawyer had a library with both federal laws and the report of federal cases* [emphasis in original]" (17).

The proposal said that Anglo lawyers were not the solution: many Mexican Americans spoke limited English and could not communicate well with Anglo lawyers. Also, some Mexican Americans said Anglo lawyers were afraid to take their cases because they feared the Anglo community might shun them. "For these reasons, Mexican-American leaders are agreed that a civil rights litigation program for Mexican-Americans can best be carried out by Mexican-American lawyers or by an organization in which they predominate" (18)

MALDEF would educate the community about their civil rights. It would provide jobs for recent law school graduates, who would train as they work.

Tijerina and his group filed their proposal and waited for Ford's decision.

CHANNELING "PROTEST ENERGY INTO LEGAL CHANNELS"

Finally, eight months after the MALDEF proposal submission, Tijerina heard back from the Ford Foundation. He was provided little information, but he was given some instructions: set up a meeting place in San Antonio—the LDF's Jack Greenberg and program officer William Pincus would come to San Antonio to give him some news.[88] Tijerina reserved a meeting room at the Gunter Hotel. This would be a public meeting, with the press invited.

The prospects looked bright: it was, of course, a positive sign that one of the foundation's top program officers and Greenberg, who had championed the concept of MALDEF through his role with the LDF, were traveling eighteen hundred miles to see Tijerina in person.

"They came and they read the letter from the Ford Foundation. They say, 'We're glad and happy to report to you that the Ford Foundation is making a grant of $2,250,000,'" Tijerina said. "Remember we had only asked for $1 million."[89]

The official letter was addressed to MALDEF president Carlos Cadena and carbon copied to Tijerina and Greenberg, from Howard R. Dresser, secretary of the Ford Foundation. There were also instructions on how some of the funds would be used. The bulk of the grant, $1.35 million, would be used for "litigation and general education activities." But additional money would also be provided:

- $100,000 for fund-raising
- $250,000 for law school scholarships for about 35 Mexican-American students "enrolled at law schools throughout the western and southwestern part of the United States."
- $500,000 for support in a sixth and seventh year of operation.[90] Alternatively, the $500,000 might fund the California Rural Legal Assistance (CRLA) program, which lost its federal funding from the Office of Economic Opportunity. MALDEF would spend some or all of the $500,000 to open an office in California.[91]

In addition to the announcement in San Antonio, the foundation also issued a seven-page news release.

"In terms of legal enforcement of their civil rights, American citizens of Mexican descent are now where the Negro community was a quarter-century ago," McGeorge Bundy, president of the foundation, was quoted in the release.[92] Bundy attributed the lag in Mexican American civil rights status to the lack of lawyers trained or financially situated to take on the cases. Also, the legal system was viewed suspiciously by many Mexican Americans, as it had been used against the best interests of Mexican Americans, and other groups. "Such factors have combined to prevent them from using the courts and other legal apparatus as affirmative instruments to secure and advance their legitimate rights.[93]

"Legal process alone will not secure civil rights, but without skillful, imaginative probes of the full potential of laws and regulations, the path to full opportunity will be harder and longer." [94]

The news release reiterated the facts from the grant proposal about unemployment and lack of legal representation and educational attainment.

"Until recently, Mexican-Americans have rarely exercised their rights of public protest, but this situation is changing. Demonstrations are likely to become more common. The Fund's leaders hope to channel the protest energy constructively into legal channels and use law as the instrument for social change," the release said.[95]

MALDEF's headquarters opened its doors on May 1, 1968, at 325 International Building, on the Mexican side of downtown San Antonio, with Pete Tijerina as the executive director, Mario Obledo as main counsel, and three staff attorneys. Its board consisted of fourteen directors.[96]

Tijerina's first attack was the Bexar County jury system and the city of San Antonio Public Service Board. "I was so angry, so full of hate," Tijerina recalled. Those were the first two lawsuits filed by MALDEF.[97]

THE SOCIAL CONTEXT OF MALDEF'S CREATION

MALDEF's first board meeting was held in the Bluebonnet Room of the Gunter Hotel in San Antonio on February 16, 1968. The board named Tijerina executive director of both the board of directors and of the legal center. It noted that Tijerina had essentially been an acting executive director since the start, handling the incipient organization's business and traveling throughout the Southwest to solicit support "at his own expense." [98] Tijerina accepted the position of director.

MALDEF came into being at a time of general unrest in the United States. Riots had erupted across the country in the summer of 1967, followed by more organized and coordinated protests by the Southern Christian Leadership Conference (SCLC), the NAACP, the Student Non-violent Coordinating Committee (SNCC), and the Congress on Racial Equality.[99] In California, Cesar Chavez and Dolores Huerta led the peaceful resistance of farmworkers—mostly, but not all, Mexican Americans—for better pay and working conditions.[100] In Texas, the Texas Farmworker Union mounted its own demands. The complaints within the larger Mexican American community included some of those farmworker concerns, but they also extended to civil issues: an electoral system that disenfranchised voters and led to scant political representation, a judiciary that seemed to turn a blind eye on Mexican Americans, police brutality, and a lack of educational access and opportunities.

Some organized resistance had gained traction. In Colorado, Rodolfo "Corky" Gonzales, a former professional boxer, had organized "Los Voluntarios" in 1963 to protest police brutality. Four years later, Gonzales organized the Crusade for Justice, which sought family involvement in fighting discrimination. The crusade also coordinated the first Chicano Annual Youth Conference.[101]

But while Gonzales was protesting and organizing walkouts and major conferences in Colorado, in neighboring New Mexico another activist, Reies Lopez Tijerina, was using more antagonistic tactics. Tijerina (no relation to MALDEF's Pete Tijerina) led La Alianza Federal de Mercedes (the Federal Alliance of Land Grants), which he formed in 1963 to press Mexican American land claims. The Alianza's tactics were confrontational and controversial. In 1966, three hundred fifty Alianza supporters occupied a national forest campground and, in the standoff with authorities that followed, took two park rangers hostage but later released them. Reies Tijerina was later convicted on charges of assault and sentenced to two years in prison and five years' probation. In 1967, Reies Lopez Tijerina attempted to make a citizen's arrest of the district attorney in the Rio Arriba County Courthouse in Tierra Amarilla, New Mexico, when gunfire broke out and a jailer was wounded. After their arrest, Reies Lopez Tijerina sought MALDEF's help to defend himself and his followers.[102]

In Texas, activists took a similar antiauthoritarian stance. The Mexican American Youth Organization (MAYO) was created in March 1967 by José Ángel Gutiérrez, Mario Compean, Ignacio Pérez, Juan Patlán, and Willie Velásquez, all students at St. Mary's University in San Antonio. Initially, the plight of the farmworkers was their focal point. But they also shared "a profound sense of urgency, frustration and anger over the powerlessness and poverty of Chicanos in Texas."[103] MAYO was highly critical of existing Mexican American organizations, like LULAC and the American G.I. Forum, for "relegating young men and all women into minor supporting roles to their older, all-male leadership . . . We saw them as wanting to become assimilated into the Anglo world, thus leaving behind their Mexican roots and culture."[104] MAYO adopted an inoffensive name, Gutiérrez writes, to counter the expected negative publicity it would receive when it began to use confrontational tactics.[105] Gutiérrez said that he and other MAYO members were included in discussions with the MALDEF organizers early on, promoting inclusion of political issues. "We wanted to make sure that there were lawyers employed at MALDEF to come to our defense at a moment's notice. We wanted to make sure that there were lawyers who would take over from our political work and press our issues in the courtroom—we were eager to be plaintiffs."[106]

But the inequality that was so evident to these groups and individuals was not apparent to some within the old social order. The Anglo power structures throughout Texas and the Southwest were generally unsympathetic, if not blind, to the legacy and presence of inequality.[107] In one instance, in 1970, San Antonio mayor Walter McAllister, in a nationally televised interview, famously attributed the high poverty rates among Mexican Americans in his city to a lack of ambition. Perhaps, he said, Mexican Americans were not "as ambitiously motivated as the Anglos to get ahead financially." Reaction was immediate. The G.I. Forum and elected officials Albert Peña, Bexar County commissioner, and Pete Torres, city councilman, demanded that McAllister apologize. McAllister defended himself, saying the quote was taken out of context.[108] In another example, Governor Preston Smith was assailed by Mexican Americans who met with him in San Antonio in June 1970. One participant, José Cardenas, the superintendent of the mostly Mexican American Edgewood school district in San Antonio, asked the governor if he believed that Mexican Americans had equal opportunity in education and employment. "I have to answer that in the affirmative," Smith replied, as the crowd erupted in catcalls and hisses. Superintendent Cardenas later told journalists that obstacles facing Mexican Americans could not be overcome "as long as high officials in government feel there's no problems."[109]

In the spring of 1970, MALDEF wrote to Harold Green, superintendent of schools in Tahoka, Texas, about thirty miles outside of Lubbock, regarding complaints of mistreatment raised by Mexican American parents. Green wrote back that there was no discrimination in Tahoka. As proof it was argued that Robert Montemayor, a student, was an accomplished athlete, a class leader, a straight-A student.[110] Montemayor, who went on to graduate from nearby Texas Tech University and become an accomplished journalist, chuckled when he heard that his success was being cited as evidence of no discrimination in Tahoka. His town of about two thousand in the 1970s was about 10 percent Mexican American, 5 percent black, and the rest Anglo. Racism was pervasive: barbershops refused to cut the hair of Mexican Americans and there were separate drinking fountains. "You knew your place," Montemayor said. "The white grip on the community was pretty fundamental and hard-core."

Montemayor said he had excelled in school because his father, Augustine Montemayor, had driven him—relentlessly pushing him to do more, be better. Over time, Robert Montemayor would come to understand his father's reasoning and agree with it: a Mexican American needed to be better to be considered equal. "I often say, I grew up in West Texas, where a Mexican American had to *want* to grow up," Montemayor said. "If you didn't have a thick skin, you would get beat down pretty good." [111]

"TROUBLESOME PEOPLE"

When MALDEF opened its doors in May 1968 in the International Building in downtown San Antonio, it was already moving quickly, organizing training workshops for "corresponding attorneys" who could augment the efforts of the small five-lawyer staff.[112] Tijerina used his new grant-writing skills to leverage the Ford money. He found additional money to organize conferences bringing in some of the biggest names in civil rights.[113] He also took advantage of a federal VISTA program to bring in five law students from the Northeast, all of whom, he would recount later, were "brilliant" young men, graduates of the best law schools. By October 1968, MALDEF held its first conference on educational discrimination, with forty-one attending and prominent speakers, including Frank White, the LDF's general counsel; Derrick A. Bell Jr., of the Western Center on Law and Poverty; law professors Michael I. Sovern (later president of Columbia University); and John Coons of the University of California, Berkeley, School of Law. Tijerina soon learned that his decisions would be open to scrutiny and second-guessing from old—and new—friends and allies. When he was invited to the education conference, George Sanchez, the venerable University of Texas professor, did not conceal his disdain at the list of speakers. "Even after 45 years of professional experience in this field I am willing to spend time learning from persons of recognized competence—e.g., Ernesto Galarza, Helen Heffernan, H. K. Manuel, Julian Nava. . . . But listening to a slate of speakers, no matter how able as lawyers, on a professional subject of my special competence and on which they have no recognized record as authorities would be a waste of time," Sanchez wrote to Tijerina.[114]

Sanchez may not have appreciated that the conferences served a function besides educating the audience: it was MALDEF's way of familiarizing the speakers with the challenges facing Mexican Americans and of building allies and supporters. Three months later, MALDEF held a second conference in Los Angeles, with eighty-one participants. A third conference was held in November 1969 at the Abiquiu, New Mexico, ghost ranch. And a fourth one in Lubbock.[115] Tijerina continued to invite high-profile speakers and to bring MALDEF greater visibility in the legal world.

WE WERE NEWBORNS

MALDEF began with six staff attorneys and five VISTA volunteers. It became obvious that a major limitation was that only a few were licensed in the state as well as the federal courts—in San Antonio, only Tijerina, Mario Obledo, and Alvaro Garza were licensed at both levels. This meant that Obledo, besides supervising the docket of cases, was "having to appear in practically all cases where referral attorneys have not been available and where motions, pre-trial conferences, depositions, and trial on the merits have taken place," he reported.[116]

Finding corresponding attorneys—who could take MALDEF cases without being on staff—was not as easy for MALDEF as it was for the LDF. Board member Gregory Luna would later explain:

We were more of a small law firm that has all their expertise from within the firm rather than adopting the [strategy], like the "Ink Fund" has lawyers, coordinating lawyers, all throughout the nation. We never could work that way because, frankly, the Mexicanos that were work-[ing] with us could never wait a year for their fee. They were all so poor that we couldn't work like that. We worked and spent a lot of time and nobody paid us, we didn't eat. So, we couldn't work that through the system. We created another system that all the work . . . got done.[117]

There were eighty-three cases and complaints pending soon after MALDEF got its work under way, Obledo said. "Numerous cases have been rejected because they are fee-generating cases for private attorneys, or else, they failed to meet the basic criterion of discrimination based on ethnic origin or poverty," Obledo wrote in a report to the MALDEF board. The cases involved a broad array of issues:

- Mexican American children in Karnes City, Texas, being held over in first grade, "irrespective of their learning ability."
- Unequal schools in the Edgewood Independent School District in San Antonio.
- A man in Odessa being fired from a tire company without cause.
- A Spanish-language newspaper publisher in Raymondville, Texas, not getting a share of the local government's legal notices business.
- Mexican Americans in a Denver subdivision suing the city for lack of basic city services.
- Selective Service practice of targeting high numbers of Mexican American draftees.

Obledo wrote that class actions would be sought in most cases. But he wished to bring an important point to their attention: MALDEF's scope should be broadened beyond the Southwest. Originally, MALDEF had been conceived as an organization to serve Mexican Americans in the Southwest. But Obledo was becoming aware of the geographic mobility of his people: they were moving beyond the traditional population centers, and MALDEF was receiving reports of problems in Washington State, in Idaho, and in Florida that could not be "cast aside."

"From Texas, the Migrant worker streams into the Rockies, Northwest and Northeastern States, and subsequently some families settle in these areas. We are constantly receiving grievances from these states involving many of the problems we encounter in the Southwest," Obledo wrote.[118]

But while MALDEF worked its way through the many requests for representation and created alliances with powerful individuals and institutions, there were other troubles brewing. MALDEF soon found itself entangled in San Antonio politics and encountering demands from Chicano law students who felt entitled to equal partnership in the new organization.

It was also forced to deal with contentious cases, in particular the case involving La Alianza Federal and its leader, Reies Lopez Tijerina, regarding Spanish land grants in New Mexico. Pete Tijerina knew that the New Mexico case would be a costly one, taking years to wend its way through the court system. It would test the fledgling organization in many ways. Tijerina approached the Field Foundation, which had provided the six-thousand-dollar planning grant to write the larger Ford proposal, seeking support to cover the cost of the case. Tijerina wrote a detailed letter to Field Foundation director Leslie W. Dunbar in August 1968, explaining that "the basic claim being that their land rights under the 'Spanish-Land Grants' and 'The Treaty of Guadalupe-Hidalgo' were confiscated by the Federal Government without any compensation at all and, presently, that the Federal Government has discriminated against these people in granting grazing permits to portions of land which are claimed as community grazing lands under the 'Spanish-Land Grants.'" [119]

Dunbar apparently sought other opinions on Tijerina's request. The following month, in an internal memo to Dunbar, someone using the initials "H. S." suggested that MALDEF represent Reies Tijerina on its own — regardless of whether it received additional grant funds from Field. "It's too early for them to act like the LDF in taking only the kinds of cases they like when there are humanly urgent needs in their own bailiwick that need immediate legal attention. . . . What's MALD for, if not for the defense of Mexican-Americans in conflict with the law on ethnic grounds? [Is the idea of representing Reies Tijerina] Too radical already?" [120]

Dunbar was noncommittal when he responded to Tijerina in October. "We shall give this our best attention and I shall be in touch with you at a later date." [121]

A two-page memo prepared by the Field Foundation staff for its trustees outlined the MALDEF proposal. "It is in its first months . . . of organization and work — an inauspicious time to be confronted with cases as controversial as these. . . . Reies Tijerina and his followers are certainly troublesome people, and I do not know what are the rights and wrongs of their actions."

The foundation said Peter Tijerina was "correct in reporting to us that under the terms of their Ford grant they must concentrate on affirmative suits, and not on criminal defense." [122]

On November 27, 1968, Dunbar wrote to Tijerina that the Field Foundation would not provide the funding for the Reies Tijerina/Alianza federal court case. [123]

Another potential problem arose in San Antonio in the form of the Mexican American Youth Organization (MAYO) and a MAYO offshoot, the Mexican-American Unity Council (MAUC). MAYO, created in San Antonio in 1967, was dedicated to empowering Mexican American youth. Its tactics included high school student walkouts to demand better facilities and curricula that reflected Mexican American culture. MAYO's leadership undertook a broad campaign that included economic development

FIGURE 3.5. *Henry B. Gonzalez. Courtesy of the Briscoe Center for American History, University of Texas at Austin.*

and the creation of a *university of the barrio*. David Montejano writes that MAYO leaders "knew that they could never secure funding directly from foundations or government sources. Thus the college-educated activists began working on several grants that would create front organizations to implement the various aspects of MAYO's wide-ranging program."[124] By August 1968, MAUC had been incorporated as a tax-exempt nonprofit economic development corporation. MAUC would be the recipient of grants and funnel funds via small grants to MAYO and other groups.[125]

But the following year, MAUC ran afoul of San Antonio city leaders when MAYO vice president Mario Compean ran against the incumbent mayor, Walter McAllister. A story on page one of the *San Antonio Light* in November 1969 was headlined: "Foundation Admits Error." The error, the paper reported, was that the Ford Foundation "admitted they boo-booed" on funding MALDEF and the Mexican American Youth Organization (MAYO) "to fight for the Chicano in the Southwest." The article, based on a report in the *Washington Post*, said MAYO had backed mayoral candidate Mario Compean, who had "received so many votes that Mayor McAllister lodged a protest to the foundation pointing out MAYO dabbling in city politics." The article said that Albert Peña Jr., the Bexar

County commissioner who was also on the MALDEF board of directors, had been summoned to the foundation's New York offices, where he reportedly told officials "what they could do with all the $3 billion of the foundation's assets."[126]

Longtime Texas congressman Henry B. Gonzalez was alarmed by the militancy of the groups. He was especially rankled by the link between MAUC, MAYO, and MALDEF. MAYO founder José Ángel Gutiérrez, a "special investigator" for MALDEF, made headlines when he gave an inflammatory speech in which he called for getting rid of Anglos, "killing them, if all else fails."[127] Some Chicanos cheered Gutiérrez for aggressively declaring his—and their—rancor for the dominant society. But other Mexican Americans found the threat of violence counterproductive to the fight for equality. Others, like Congressman Gonzalez, were apoplectic. It was clear that MAYO was financially dependent on MALDEF and another Ford Foundation–funded organization, the Southwest Council of La Raza. Gonzalez met with Herman Gallegos, the executive director of the Southwest Council of La Raza, and with Ford Foundation staffers in Washington on September 9, 1969, regarding what Gonzalez said was "a lack of communication and control between your office, your board and your San Antonio grantees." He criticized MAUC for a "lack of judgment and maturity. . . . There comes a point when any man must speak out in his own defense, and against activities which threaten the community."[128]

Gonzalez acquired a copy of Gutiérrez's 1968 master's thesis, entitled: "La Raza and Revolution: The Empirical Conditions of Revolution in Four South Texas Counties." The young Chicano leader's basic premise was that, with pervasive inequality and discrimination, there was bound to be a revolt.[129] Gutiérrez wrote that a path had already been hewn through the earlier successes in Crystal City:

> For years the conditions in South Texas have been strikingly similar to Latin America. Exploitation and oppression of the Mexican American has been going on for years. With the recent developments in the Mexican American movement that have been brought about a sense of group identity, solidarity, and desire for change, the Mexican Americans are not only acutely aware of their dilemma and misery, but are engaging in social action. The Mexican American movement is within the framework of a genuine social movement. . . .
>
> Crystal City aroused the sentiments of the nation. The movement now has aroused the sentiments of the Mexican Americans themselves. Could the way to change the existing conditions be revolution?[130]

Gonzalez could not tolerate what he regarded as a threat. On April 3, 1969, Gonzalez made a speech on the floor of Congress, characterizing the Ford Foundation as "by far the greatest of all foundations dedicated to the advancement of humanity" and one that had attempted to alleviate the hardships of Mexican Americans "who have suffered long and endured much." But, Gonzalez said, the foundation's grants to groups in San Antonio had produced "a very grave problem." He aimed his attacks on the Southwest Council of La Raza, which had received a $630,000 grant from the Ford Foundation, as well as at MALDEF.

> The Ford Foundation believed that the greatest need of this particular minority group was to have some kind of effective national organization that could coordinate the actions of the many that already existed, and give for once an effective and united voice to this minority group. This good desire may have rested on a false assumption; namely that such a disparate group could, any more than our black brothers or our white "Anglo" brothers, be brought under one large tent. There are conflicting interests in any group of any race or creed, and this must be recognized. Whatever the case may be, the Ford Foundation established the Southwest Council of La Raza and gave it a treasury of $630,000.

The Southwest Council, in turn, made a grant of $110,000 to the Mexican-American Unity Council of San Antonio, Gonzalez said. And the Unity Council's only work entailed creating other groups: one for parents, another for neighborhoods, a third dedicated to voter registration. And the Unity Council had given money to the "militant Mexican-American Youth Organization—MAYO."

> There is no reason whatever to believe that for all the money this group has spent, there is any understanding of what it is actually being spent for, except to employ friends of the director and advance his preconceived notion. The people who are to be united apparently don't get much say in what the "unity council" is up to.
> As an example, the president of MAYO is not on the Unity Council payroll; but he is on the payroll of another Ford Foundation group, the Mexican-American Legal Defense Fund. He is an investigator but appears to spend his time on projects not related to his defense work. This handy device enables him to appear independent of Foundation activities and still make a living from the Foundation. Of course, his MAYO speeches denigrating the "gringos" and calling for their elimina-

tion by "killing them if all else fails" do little for unity, and nothing for law, but that bothers neither him nor his associates.

I fear very much that the Ford Foundation miscalculated in choosing those who have charge over their grant money.[131]

Gonzalez went further. David Montejano writes that Gonzalez also met with Wilbur Mills, chairman of the House Ways and Means Committee, and with Wright Patman, chairman of the House Banking Committee, both of whom were already engaged in reviewing the tax-exempt privileges of charitable foundations. The Texas congressman "did his best to contain the movement, and these efforts at first glance appeared successful," Montejano writes.[132]

In 1969, Pete Tijerina fired José Ángel Gutiérrez. But Gutiérrez was not one to walk away quietly. "I got plenty [mad] and told him [Tijerina] how gutless he was for bending to Ford." Tijerina relented somewhat and agreed to keep Gutiérrez on salary until the end of his contract in the fall.[133]

Gonzalez worked in other ways to undermine MALDEF and its leaders, setting his sights on, among others, Texas state senator Joe Bernal, who was pursuing a doctorate in education from the University of Texas at Austin. Gonzalez wrote to the dean of the College of Arts and Sciences, John R. Silber, that there were reports that Bernal was receiving academic credit for his "professional work, and also for certain aspects of his political work," in order to curry favor with his advisor, George I. Sanchez. "[W]hat distresses me is the claim that any candidate would be given academic credit for non-academic work." Gonzalez closed by assuring Silber that his interest was in "preserving the integrity of the University."[134] Later, university officials assured Gonzalez that Bernal's work would require the approval of a committee of professors, as was true for all doctoral students.[135]

Gonzalez's public attacks on MALDEF were met with a flurry of letters to his office and to newspapers. Other nationally prominent Mexican American leaders treaded gingerly. Three of them, the country's only other Mexican American congressman, Ed Roybal; the country's only Mexican American U.S. senator, Joseph Montoya of New Mexico; and Vicente Ximenes, a member of the U.S. Equal Opportunity Employment Commission and the head of the Cabinet Committee on Mexican American Affairs, wrote a short letter to the Ford Foundation, supporting MALDEF, without addressing any of the controversies that were swirling around it.[136]

FIGURE 3.6. *Joe Bernal, 2006. Courtesy of the Voces Oral History Project. Photo by Valentino Mauricio.*

Other indications of how Gonzalez's actions were perceived are letters he received from Mexican American activists in Texas and in other states, calling him a *"vendido"* (sellout) and worse. For these people, Gonzalez, who by this time had been in Congress for eight years, but had earlier served on the San Antonio City Council (1953–1956) and in the Texas state senate (1957–1961), had lost touch with the problems of common Mexican Americans. One letter to the editor in the *San Antonio Express-News* was representative. The writer, Gilbert Rice, said that in 1949, Gonzalez had been a civil rights fighter, successfully fighting segregation. But in 1969, Gonzalez was being counterproductive:

> Henry's 1949 methods for social change have been proved useless and inadequate. He has no right to impose the use of his antiquated 1949 methods in 1969 because conditions for the chicano have not changed appreciably in the past 20 years in Texas and the Southwest. 1949's snail's pace is for the birds. . . . The choice for chicanos is not between MAYO and a congressman who apparently considers himself to be a super-Mexican, above reproach or criticism. The choice is between 1969 and 1949. The choice for all chicanos is to either remain stagnant as a people—bowing and scraping before gringos for 20 more years, or uniting in massive numbers and moving forward—at all costs—to secure and safeguard equal rights, full opportunity and full citizenship for all our chicano brothers.[137]

Beyond Texas, Gonzalez's actions were also condemned. One Los Angeles–based Chicano newsletter detailed the congressman's meetings with the Ford Foundation, his denunciation of the Mexican American organizations, and Ford's subsequent actions.

> Perhaps it is not possible for HBG and his $42,500 and prestige position to understand what it is to hurt any longer. He does not remember nor understand that MAYO cannot and has not created division, ill will or injustice. The division existed long before any of the young MAYO members were born. As a matter of fact, it was created over 100 years ago and the end product of that division: poverty, illiteracy and 3rd class citizenship continues unabated.[138]

Gonzalez's stance on issues of race was complicated. He was un-questioningly proud of his roots, but refused to come to the defense of

Mexican American constituents who claimed unequal treatment. He was elected to represent his district, including non-Mexican Americans, he said repeatedly. "I am not a professional Mexican," he wrote to one man who had asked for his intervention on a matter of employment discrimination. "I have never presented myself as a power broker for what you call the Mexican-American people, but as a representative of all the people. If what you want is a power broker, then you will have to find someone else, because my experience has been that it is the brokers of power, operating in the name of people of Spanish surname, who have done the greatest damage to the progress of this ethnic group, simply by selling out at the highest bid." [139]

The true measure of how Gonzalez was perceived after the intense MALDEF debacle came in the following election cycle, when he was reelected to represent District 20 in Congress: no opponents challenged him.

SCHOLARSHIP FUND

The scholarship fund also emerged as a problem for MALDEF. The original Ford grant earmarked $250,000 for scholarships for "about 35 students." But when the opportunity became public, MALDEF was inundated with applications and Tijerina could not bring himself to turn away promising and committed students. Wishing to do more with that amount, Tijerina amplified the program—contacting law school deans and securing agreements from them to match the MALDEF scholarship. MALDEF also produced a fund-raising brochure, listing the participating law schools, the board of directors, the scholarship committee, and the scholarship advisory committee. In the brochure, MALDEF distanced itself from Chicano radicals: "Aware of the tragic consequences of unbridled militancy, MALDEF initiated a Legal Education Program to bring promising and committed students into the legal profession where they will be able to make significant contributions toward improving the lives of their people." [140]

Finally, MALDEF provided scholarships to 118 students, three times as many as the foundation had anticipated, and turning down about as many for lack of funds. [141]

To raise additional funds, Tijerina sent a four-page letter to the Ford Foundation, seeking donations, telling them that "a gift of $2,000 which will be matched by a participating law school, will provide one year's tuition and living costs for a needy Mexican American student pursuing a legal education."

The letter appeared to be a form letter, sent to other foundations and perhaps corporations and individuals. It would seem so, as much of the letter outlines the need for Mexican American civil rights lawyers—facts that the Ford Foundation would be intimately aware of—and it was addressed simply to "The Ford Foundation," with a simple salutation of "Gentlemen." The foundation may have wondered why Tijerina would be asking for $2,000 after it had given him $250,000 for the scholarships. Ford officials may have been concerned that Tijerina was concentrating so much of his energy on augmenting what was a generous stipend to begin with. And the program officers must have been alarmed when they read that MALDEF intended an "accelerating program," announcing, "By September 1973, we hope to have 500 first year students, 350 second year students, and 300 third year students, for a total of 1,150 Mexican-American students attending law school with financial support from MALDEF and matching scholarships from the individual schools." [142] The logistics of administering such a suddenly expanding program, while ensuring quality and follow-through, would undoubtedly be problematic. Tijerina was nervous about submitting the scholarship program report after its first year: "You will probably find something wrong with it, but be assured that your suggestions will be considered and the Report revised in accordance therewith." [143]

But the problem that the foundation had with the report was less about the style, but more on what Tijerina had done—committing the entire grant amount in the first year rather than proceeding at a more measured pace. Also, Tijerina had spent considerable time securing the cooperation of the law school deans. Continuing the scholarship would require maintaining and amplifying those law school relationships. It would also require Tijerina to undertake a sustained, major fund-raising effort for the scholarships, at a time when MALDEF was also expected to raise operating funds for its core mission. Ford Foundation program officer Leonard E. Ryan wrote to Tijerina on April 24, 1970, acknowledging receipt of the scholarship report and calling the support of 113 students "an accomplishment." But, Ryan added, "We do recommend that the future of the scholarship program be carefully deliberated with the scholarship advisory committee. The members of that committee can be of great help." [144]

The scholarship program caught the attention of a group of Chicano law students who demanded control of the scholarship fund and a voice within MALDEF as well. In July 1970, the La Raza National Law Students met with Mario Obledo, MALDEF's general counsel, and Albert Armendariz, the MALDEF board president, and presented the two men with a long list of the student group's demands. In the days that followed, the student group sent a two-page memo—in aggressive all-capital letters—to the MALDEF directors, outlining their demands in the form of resolutions that had been approved unanimously by the student group. Top of the list was that MALDEF add ten more directors, selected from the student group, to its twenty-person board. It also said that the student group wanted complete control over the scholarship fund. The student group could "RELIEVE MALD OF THE ADDITIONAL BURDEN IT HOLDS IN THE ADMINISTRATION OF THE SCHOLARSHIP PROGRAM. . . . LET IT BE RESOLVED THAT: MALDEF TURN OVER THE COMPLETE CONTROL OF THE MALDEF SCHOLARSHIP FUND TO LRNLSA AND ALL POWERS NECESSARY TO EFFECTUATE AND MAXIMIZE THE PROGRAM."[145]

The La Raza student group also sought MALDEF's financial support to cover the student group's organizational expenses and the recruitment of more Chicano law students, and it sought to increase the number of law schools with special admissions programs.[146]

MALDEF board president Albert Armendariz took the students' demands seriously and dashed off letters to the board members, calling a special meeting on August 2, 1970, in Tucson, to discuss the matter. The following day, he sent each member photocopies of the student group's demands.

Response by board members was swift. In a tersely worded letter to Armendariz, board member Louis Garcia of San Francisco called the student demands "unreasonable irrespective of the fact that they may be future attorneys. Let them act as future attorneys." Garcia said he had met earlier with the students in Berkeley, where they made the same demands. The student attempt to assume control of the scholarship fund "is highly unreasonable," Garcia said. If the Ford Foundation wished to, it could make grants to the student group, he said. "This money was granted by the Ford Foundation to MALDEF and how it can be conceived that we can now turn it over to another organization is beyond my powers of comprehension.

"The request for 10 students as members on the Board is extremely unreasonable even if the by-laws permitted it, and they should have been advised accordingly," Garcia wrote. "If you think that they will stop with these demands wait until they have 10 Board members."[147]

Los Angeles board member Richard A. Ibañez also responded immediately, making three points:

1. The directors could not "abdicate and let the students take over even if we wanted to."
2. The appropriate course of action in situations such as these was for a MALDEF committee to deliberate these issues "before matters are presented to the entire board for action."
3. A scholarship committee had already developed a procedure for the selection of board members. "I do not want to by-pass the clear thinking and excellent work done on this subject by Lou Garcia."[148]

Armendariz reversed direction and agreed with Ibañez and Garcia, apparently a little bit embarrassed at having been caught up in the moment.[149]

With so many negative headlines about MAYO's involvement, the Gonzalez diatribe on the floor of Congress, and a scholarship program apparently reeling out of control, the Ford Foundation stepped in. By the end of November 1970, the foundation had notified Tijerina and board chairman Armendariz that a three-person team would be visiting the MALDEF offices on January 4–7, 1971, to make a general review and evaluation of the performance and progress of the fund's activities, including administration, the scholarship program, fund-raising and management of the grant funds." Leonard Ryan, the foundation's grant advisor for MALDEF, assured Tijerina that the review was "customary after such a grant has been running for a substantial period of time."[150]

THE BOMBSHELL

The following week, at a regularly scheduled Washington, D.C., meeting, MALDEF board members sat down to what they were expecting to be a routine work meeting. But in the next several minutes, they would be handed what Chairman Albert Armendariz would call "a bombshell" that would call for substantial changes to the organization.

That afternoon, Armendariz called the meeting to order and a motion was made, seconded, and passed that the regular order of business be suspended to hear from three Ford Foundation officers.[151] Pete Tijerina excused himself.

Christopher F. Edley, the officer in charge of the government and law section, under the Division of National Affairs,[152] told the board that the foundation had shared some of the recommendations with the executive committee. The recommendations were sweeping, dealing with a reorganization and a relocation. Tijerina's position, as executive director, would be eliminated, and the top position would be that of general counsel. The makeup of the board should be such as to include one-third non-Mexican Americans and should also include members who were not lawyers; board members would be approved by the foundation as well. The bylaws of MALDEF should be updated to reflect the reality of what the organization had become.

The national headquarters should be moved from San Antonio, with "serious consideration [to] be given to relocating the National Headquarters in Washington, D.C., or Denver, Colorado. The Ford Foundation would like to concur in the new location of the office." After the move, there should be field offices in San Antonio, Los Angeles, and in New Mexico, Arizona, and Colorado.

In response to questions, the Ford representatives said that the use of the term *national headquarters* did not mean to imply that there should be a change in concept. "When the grant was made we assumed a national organization but we are flexible on this and it is up to the Board to decide whether you want to be a national organization," the Ford officials said, according to the text of a transcript of the meeting.[153]

Board members worried that the relocation would cut into MALDEF's budget: *Would Ford defray expenses required by the relocation?* Answer: "Ford Foundation has a practice of not supplementing grants until money already expanded [*sic*] has all been spent."

But, the Ford representative said, it is possible for the grant to be spent in a shorter period of time, and, when those funds were exhausted, MALDEF could apply for refunding. There was no assurance that more Ford money would be forthcoming: "We did not invest this kind of money and leave it to change overnight. It is risky. You are not falling flat on your faces but should you do, we have to maintain a procedure. We prefer the recommendation that whether it comes at the end of 4 or 5 years, the result will be based on merit," an unidentified Ford representative said in the transcript.

From the transcript, it is apparent that board members were caught by surprise. Chairman Armendariz confirmed that discussions with the Ford representatives the previous night "included only the discussion of the possible move and . . . these recommendations came as a complete surprise."

Perhaps the only MALDEF representative who was expecting the ultimatum was Pete Tijerina, who later told reporters he had been called to the foundation's New York office the week before and was told changes would be made—or else Ford's funding would dry up.[154] But the board members were caught off guard. Indications had been that MALDEF was moving positively at a fast clip, one member (not identified in the transcript) told the Ford representatives. "One report from [the] NAACP stated that they were astonished at the amount of [cases filed] by MALDEF. He thought we had moved quite rapidly. We were able to accomplish in 1 year what had taken the Black Communities 10 years."

The Ford staff responded that they had not completed an evaluation of the legal work that had been undertaken by the MALDEF offices.

What, the board asked, *would happen if the board rejected the foundation's recommendations?* "The Foundation has the power to cancel, reduce, suspend or not to review," a Ford officer said. "I would not be the person in the Foundation making the decision in regards to that."

After the Ford representatives left the room, the board scrambled to find its footing—there were several issues to consider, many unanswered questions; in fact, many questions had yet to be formulated. The first issue was the relocation of the office. If it stayed in the Southwest, where should it be located? The board debated the advantages and disadvantages of each possibility—grappling for the essence of the challenges facing the Mexican American people, the strengths and the weaknesses within the community.

Moving the headquarters to Washington had some attraction: it would be close to the federal seat of power, closer to the major news media outlets. "We have no establishment in the mind of the national news media," lamented Henry "Hank" Lopez.

But Dan Sosa of New Mexico responded that MALDEF would be competing for attention with other major organizations. "We would probably get lost in a shuffle," Sosa said. "I do not know what would be wrong in keeping it in the Southwest. That is where the action is."

But, Lopez insisted, D.C. would be preferable: any location in the Southwest would mean butting up against local Chicano politics, an apparent reference to what had happened in San Antonio.

Roger Cisneros agreed that "the Eastern part of the country is the one that makes the decisions," but he would opt for Denver. Corky Gonzales of the Crusade for Justice could be helpful.

An office in Washington did not ensure that MALDEF would escape the line of fire; rather than local detractors, it would have congressional critics, said Louie Garcia. Washington, D.C., made sense for the African American community, as there was a substantial African American population there. For Mexican Americans, "you do not have any organizations in Washington to get community involvement," Garcia said. Also, the Northeast was identified more as Puerto Rican territory, said Garcia. Having MALDEF in the Southwest would be "identifying to the Mexican-American."

Several board members agreed that the Southwest had a strong pull. It was, after all, the "homeland," the symbolic and historical home of the Mexican American community—where the vast majority resided and where their problems were most marked. There was much to be said for "legal involvement that can be done out in the field," said Louie Garcia. Richard Ibañez of Los Angeles agreed that the Southwest was the "battlefield." If MALDEF moved to Washington, the danger was that "we may lose the sensitivity to the problems. We would lose our effectiveness as foot soldiers that are fighting a war," Ibañez said. On the other hand, he added, it would likely be easier to attract funding in D.C.

There was some face-saving needed, too. Pete Tijerina, who had apparently rejoined the group, weighed in. "My only opposition to Washington is because it was their [Ford's] idea. . . . It has to be a counter proposal."

Chairman Armendariz signaled he was relieved by the board's discussion. He "had foreseen an angry discussion in that Ford was telling us what to do—'Machismo.' . . . We have been able to sit and in harmony deal with our position in this matter. I think that is a sign that we may be growing up." [155]

The board voted to let the executive committee review the Ford Foundation's recommendations and to get back to the board with their assessment.

After returning to San Antonio, Tijerina chose to draw attention to the Ford Foundation's ultimatum. He called a press conference on Tuesday, March 17, at La Louisiane restaurant, telling reporters about the turn of events, which was described by the *San Antonio Light* as "an ultimatum." The *Light* quoted Tijerina as saying that the Ford Foundation said there was "too much political turmoil associated with the organization in

San Antonio and Los Angeles. . . . [T]hey mentioned no names, but I am sure they were referring to our organization's association with people like [state] Sen. Joe Bernal and county commissioner Albert Peña." Tijerina said the foundation had insisted on seeing that neither Bernal nor Peña was receiving foundation funds before it would release its quarterly grant payment.

Tijerina also said that MALDEF's support of MAYO "might have had some bearing on the case." [156]

The MALDEF turmoil occupied the front pages of the San Antonio newspapers for some time. On March 18, 1970, Congressman Gonzalez was quoted in a local newspaper saying he had not sought contact with any foundation about MALDEF in 1970, but that the Ford people had reached out to him after he made several speeches on "The New Racism." The foundation's responsibility, Gonzalez said, did not end at providing funds: "[T]hey have a continuing responsibility to see that it is used constructively and not destructively—like putting enormous amounts of money into the hands of young, inexperienced and completely misdirected persons." [157]

Albert Peña, who had missed the Washington meeting with the foundation, called his own press conference and told reporters that MALDEF's problems were caused by "the Washington mad man," a clear reference to Gonzalez: "He has vowed in concert with [Mayor W. W.] McAllister forces many times that he will destroy MALDEF and the civil rights movement in San Antonio and that he will see to it that Pete Tijerina was sacked. He may succeed in moving MALDEF out of San Antonio and he already has succeeded in getting Pete [Tijerina] fired but he will neither destroy the Chicano civil rights movement nor MALDEF." [158]

Asked if he was referring to Congressman Gonzalez, Peña replied: "there is only one mad man in Washington." [159]

In response to Peña's assertions, Tijerina issued a press release the following day, countering that he had not been "sacked" but that his position had, instead, been eliminated. Tijerina also said his only problem with Peña was that he was absent from the meeting in Washington.

Sometime in April 1970, Pete Tijerina formalized his resignation as MALDEF's executive director, effective immediately, giving Mario Obledo the latitude to reorganize MALDEF. Tijerina's letter was straightforward and positive, with no hint of the difficulties that led to his resignation. "It has been for me a gratifying experience to strive for attaining the purposes of MALDEF as it is now to turn over the leadership to a person as qualified and dedicated as Mario is." [160] Richard A. Ibañez, chairman of MALDEF's executive committee, accepted Tijerina's resignation, recognizing that "it is upon your efforts and successes that we start on the new job of expanding the program of MALDEF. Without them we would not now be."[161]

Greenberg later would credit Tijerina for providing "the spark that got MALDEF under way."[162]

EPILOGUE

MALDEF moved its headquarters to San Francisco and was operating there as of January 1, 1971, with General Counsel Mario Obledo, five other attorneys, a development officer, an administrative assistant, and five secretaries.[163] MALDEF's concern with how its actions were to be perceived—both by the larger Mexican American community as well as by the foundation—would continue to weigh on the board. One problem that emerged centered on a board meeting in Mexico City, intended to entice members who might otherwise not come. Los Angeles attorney and board member Herman Sillas wrote to Leonard Ryan in February 1971 that he was "disturbed" that the April board meeting would be held in Mexico City.

> We are constantly under attack by the Activists in the community
> who claim we are not doing enough for the Mexican community. This
> is nothing more than a direct result of the frustration of the community
> wherein the problems are numerous and the organizations few.
> ... [W]e would only compound our problems with our relationship
> with the Mexican community once they became aware that the Board
> of Directors saw fit to fly to Mexico City to discuss the problems of the
> Mexican-American in the United States.[164]

Sillas also worried about spending funds for "luxuries for members of the Board" rather than "the hiring of additional staff which is greatly needed." Sillas noted that one reason given for the Mexico City meeting was to "entice" board members to attend. "I believe as dedicated Board Members, we do not need an enticement to attend a Board Meeting and perform our duty and accept our responsibilities." He urged board members to contact the executive committee and urge it to reconsider the Mexico City site. "[P]olitically the holding of the next Board Meeting in Mexico City would make it very difficult for myself and the staff members working on MALDEF to face the community and tell it that MALDEF is concerned with its problems," Sillas wrote.[165]

In spite of Sillas's objections, the meeting was held in Mexico as planned, amid great fanfare and media coverage by the Mexican press.

Records show that the new general counsel, Mario Obledo, made several administrative improvements. But in 1970, an outside evaluator found there was still some polishing needed. In 1971, the Stanford University professor Paul Brest outlined what he saw were shortcomings:

1. Unclear priorities. ("Not only does it not have priorities among affirmative litigation goals, but it lacks clear priorities between affirmative civil rights litigation and community service activities. The San Francisco office stresses civil rights litigation; the Los Angeles office focuses on community service; and the San Antonio office seems only now—after much prodding by Mario—to be doing anything visible.")[166]
2. Referral attorney performance inconsistent. ("As with the NAACP-LDF the quality of work by referral attorneys is inconsistent.")[167]

Brest recommended that MALDEF's Program and Planning Committee develop guidelines for the organization and that referral attorneys be monitored more closely by staff attorneys. He also urged the foundation to "put the screws on the hard-nosed lawyer board members to take a more active role in defining MALDEF's goals and operational procedures and supervising the organization."[168] And he closed with some sensitivity to MALDEF's independence and his own ambiguous relationship to the fledgling organization: "I am in no position to push: I don't think you intend me to act as Mario's boss [Obledo, the chief counsel], and if I tried it would ruin whatever relationship I have established with MALDEF."[169]

Brest followed up with an assessment of MALDEF's scholarship program, noting that the scholarships to law students were either five hundred or a thousand dollars, with the law schools expected to match the amount. Brest said the procedure is "running smoothly, and would be capable of handling a substantially larger grant budget than it presently has."[170]

Obledo, in a March 1971 letter to Ford Foundation president McGeorge Bundy, highlighted the organization's successes: courtroom victories, out-of-court settlements, 137 Chicano law students funded at 23 law schools. "No case has been completely lost," Obledo wrote. "Social change has been an inevitable result of even adverse decisions . . . Thus, the investment which the Foundation made in the Mexican American community has brought orderly social change and human progress. The Chicano has reached the threshold of equality. With continued effort he will gain that elusive goal." [171]

Obledo's tenure was also short-lived. He opened the San Francisco national headquarters in 1971, but, it was noted, his wife and family had moved back to San Antonio, and Ford officials believed he would be following them soon.

There were no women on the first board of directors, but two female Mexican American attorneys were named to the 1971 board: Graciela Olivarez and Vilma Martinez Singer. Martinez had deep connections: she was a native San Antonian and a graduate of the University of Texas (which Pete Tijerina, Carlos Cadena, and several other founding board members had also attended). After graduating in 1967 from Columbia Law School (also Greenberg's alma mater), she went to work as a staff attorney at the LDF. Martinez became MALDEF's president and general counsel from 1973 to 1982. Under Martinez, MALDEF organized a Chicana Rights Project and further professionalized the organization by creating staff guides and guidelines and instituting new policies. Joaquin Avila served from 1982 to 1985. He was succeeded by Antonia Hernandez, who would serve from 1985 to 2003.

But even as MALDEF gained courtroom successes within its first decade, it found new stumbling blocks. After a case was won, there remained an "enormous gap" between the court decree and the "actual situation," Martinez said in a proposal to the New World Foundation in 1975. Martinez said that MALDEF's substantial litigation successes were not the end of the story: MALDEF was compelled repeatedly to take action to ensure that those remedies would be implemented.[172]

Martinez outlined MALDEF's strengths and achievements. One key development was that the organization no longer relied on a single foundation for its funding. Its annual budget was over $750,000, with donations and grants from sources that included IBM and the Rockefeller Foundation—"another indication of its respectability," Martinez wrote.[173] It had seventeen staff attorneys and had scored "victory upon victory, most notably, perhaps, in the areas of educational opportunity and political access." [174] MALDEF had assumed a leadership position as experts in several subjects, "such as the recent passage in the House of the Voting Rights Act which is heralded as a most important piece of civil rights litigation, extending to the Spanish-speaking minority in various parts of the

Southwest the same privileges of political access which Southern blacks fought to gain for themselves in the mid-1960s." [175]

Martinez's purpose in writing to the New World Foundation was to propose the creation of a Community Education and Community Activation Program, focusing on four issues: bilingual education; political access and voting rights; census and other types of data collection; and areas that might involve federal government funding. The effort would entail providing information, training, and sharing of resources with community groups, a way to "create a sufficient level of sophistication and a sufficient level of information and analytical ability so that Chicano community groups can earn for themselves their due place in the struggle for civil liberties and civil rights.

> You asked me to defend why MALDEF—a group of lawyers, after all— should be doing this. Upon reflection, I think the best answer to that is that MALDEF perhaps should not be doing this—but it must. As I think you understand, the Chicano community has not yet organized itself effectively to insure its entitlements and to receive the benefits to which it is entitled. There are relatively few organized Chicano groups who work at a community level to insure the receipt of our rights and entitlements; and those that do exist have looked to MALDEF and in general have received MALDEF's help.

Martinez wrote that she envisioned this program as short term, a three-year effort.

"If, at the end of that time, we have not activated community groups to fight in their own behalf for that which is their right, then we have failed and we should terminate." [176]

Eight years after its launch, MALDEF had found that it was, in fact, ahead of its community—as the labor economist and farmworker activist Ernesto Galarza had predicted in 1967.

In 2008, MALDEF celebrated its fortieth anniversary and produced a video that included details of its history, crediting Tijerina for his central role in creating the organization and including an interview with the Ford Foundation's new president, a Latino named Luis Urbiñas. Urbiñas said the foundation was proud to have worked with MALDEF on a variety of issues, including education, immigration, and voting rights. "Those are the kinds of things that Ford has to support," Urbiñas said.

In its annual report for that year, MALDEF noted that the need for its services had not abated. MALDEF had adopted the broader term "Latino" in place of Mexican American, to reflect the increase in different ethnic groups, other than Mexican American.[177] And, as the Latino population grows, so, too have civil rights challenges, particularly revolving around immigration and political representation. The cause of fully incorporating the Mexican American and, more broadly, the Latino population into the social fabric of the country had become increasingly urgent: demographers predicted that by 2050, Hispanics will compose 29 percent of the nation's population.[178]

MALDEF's fund-raising efforts have become sophisticated. It holds gala dinners in major cities; its November 2011 Los Angeles dinner included awards to superstars: the singer Linda Ronstadt and former MAL-DEF president Antonia Hernandez. And it featured presentations by the Mexican singer Pepe Aguilar and the actress Eva Longoria. The lowest priced tickets were $175; sponsorships were as high as $75,000. MALDEF fund-raisers rely on local attorneys—of all ethnicities—and major corporations to help cover the organization's expenses. It no longer relies on only one funding source. MALDEF appeals to anyone who believes in Mexican American civil rights to contribute what they can; its website's donation page has radial buttons that go from $5 to $250.

Asking a sympathetic public to donate is not a new development for MALDEF. In 1975, when Joe Bernal wrote to then MALDEF chairman Richard A. Ibañez, he underscored the importance of the Ford Foundation's support. But, he said, the Mexican American community was simply getting its just due. "[T]o a very large extent they [foundations] owed us that effort. Foundations managing money to assist worthy causes, money which would have ordinarily gone to support our government, had not been made available to our 'forgotten Americans' as Sanchez called us or to the 'invisible minority' as others tagged us."

It was time now, Bernal said, for the Mexican American community to step up and support MALDEF, to endorse MALDEF's good work by dipping into individual pocketbooks. "The work that MALDEF has been doing for our communities and barrios throughout the United States merits that support," he wrote.

And with that, Bernal enclosed a twenty-dollar check, an installment toward his hundred-dollar pledge. And he signed it, c/s—*con safos*—the Chicano slang for "with respect."[179]

Conclusion

OF ORAL HISTORY AND
RESEARCH POSSIBILITIES

In the final section of their 2012 study on the Ford Foundation's relations with Chicano intellectuals, Victoria-Maria MacDonald and Benjamin Polk Hoffman note that the field of Chicano history relies on interviews and other primary sources. "While Julian Samora's history is being preserved at the Julian Samora Institute, this is also a call for more interviews with members of the Chicano movement while they are available as living documents," the researchers write.[1] The need for quality interviews and other documentation of the experiences and lives of U.S. Latinos has been recognized throughout the country, and fortunately people have busily collected as many quality interviews and papers as possible.[2]

The first two of these chapters could not have been written without those oral history interviews, what one activist, the Chicano historian Juan Gómez Quiñones, calls "an indispensable source."[3] As is demonstrated here, the written record—particularly about the El Paso Police and Fire Departments—is painfully sparse. But even when there are ample archival materials to ground the study, the voices of the men and women who lived the experience impart the fundamental human dimension, putting a face on the writings about the past. One conclusion, reached by many before now, is the importance for Latinos to leave a record of their experience: letters; diaries; photographs that include the story of who, what, when, and where; memoirs; newsletters; event programs; invitations; and so forth. All of these items help reveal the past and are helpful to researchers. (The Society of American Archivists offers guidance on how to preserve materials at their website: http://www2.archivists.org /node/7978.)

These three studies have revealed yet more areas that might yet be mined: questions of class, leadership, geographic mobility, geographic stereotypes, and methods of protesting. One key theme that runs through all three of these chapters is the issue of social capital and class; in some instances, relating to education. For example, in the study of the Alpine schools, Pete Gallego Sr. and Elena Gallego had both earned bachelor's degrees at Sul Ross. Pete Gallego Sr. used the G.I. Bill to finance his education. His education and veteran status were not the only attributes that marked Pete Gallego as a potential leader: his family was already respected and well-established in the community because of his parents' restaurant, the Green Café. But at a time when college was unattainable for many Mexican Americans, his educational background instantly enhanced his credentials as a school board candidate.

In the case of Raymond L. Telles in El Paso, class and social capital was in some ways a larger factor. He had attended a business school. But Telles was more attractive because he had attended Cathedral High School, the well-regarded boys Catholic school in town, and because he was a military veteran. His parents belonged to the Círculo Mexicano, "the most exclusive social club for Mexicans in El Paso, composed largely of prominent families who had found refuge in the border city during the Mexican Revolution," according to biographer Mario T. García.[4] Beyond that, both his father, Ramón, and younger brother, Richard, were politically active and shrewd. There were other men with some of Raymond Telles's same characteristics. But his family's ties undoubtedly provided that initial push and a campaign infrastructure that another candidate may not have enjoyed. How have other Latinos built on their own networks to run for political office? What advantages/disadvantages might Latinos have that others don't?

Comparing and contrasting geographic differences is another area ripe for study. When Pete Tijerina visits New Mexico in 1967, evangelizing about what will become the Mexican American Legal Defense and Educational Fund, he is corrected: "'Mr. Tijerina, we're not Mexican Americans in New Mexico; we're Spanish Americans,'" Tijerina would say later with amusement.[5] The geographic differentials arose again when Tijerina was told that the West Coast lawyers "didn't want any damned Mexicanos from Texas telling Mexicanos from California what to do."[6]

In interviews with other World War II veterans, California veterans often characterize Texas Mexican Americans as less educated and less sophisticated. Texas veterans often say their California counterparts were more assimilated and often spoke no Spanish. Some Mexican Americans outside of New Mexico are curious—and skeptical—about the Hispano tradition in both New Mexico and Colorado. Although there were alli-ances established, members of each group were initially suspicious of one another. From whence did the perceptions derive? How much was true? What were the effects? How does it compare to today's Latinos?

On a related note: it has been noted that World War II ushered in large-scale urbanization in general. More than 80 percent of Mexican Americans lived in urban areas by 1960. The urbanization of Texas's Mexican American population was addressed by David Montejano in his 1987 book, *Anglos and Mexicans in the Making of Texas, 1836–1986*. Further analysis of that demographic is called for, including interviews with men and women who experienced it personally, who could relate how moving from rural homes to urban areas changed family, identity, and commu-nity. For instance, in one 1999 interview, Ramón Rivas described grow-ing up on the family farm, with no alarm clocks to awaken him and his brother. He just woke up when the sun rose, he said.[7]

In several exchanges with World War II–era Latinos and Latinas, they have emphasized that they were able to accomplish change quietly—a point of contention with their offspring in the Chicano movement who used public protest to secure civil rights. And in fact, that tension— between the "radical" Chicanos pushing for immediate change and the more measured steps taken by generally older Mexican Americans—is present in all three of the case studies. The distaste for protests is in-cluded in the Ford Foundation's announcement of the $2.2 million MAL-DEF grant in 1968. It said the creation of the new organization, MALDEF, would "channel the protest energy constructively into legal channels and use law as the instrument for social change."[8]

In another example, in a 2002 interview Leon Eguía in Houston re-called how his cohort had gone about opening doors to police and fire departments in the 1950s:

> In 1953, I was the president of LULAC Council 60. We were fight-ing the city, the county, on discrimination, because they wouldn't hire no Latinos in the fire department and the police department. . . . At that time, we had an activist, he was a writer for the *Houston Press* . . . name of Sandy Anderson, and he helped us a lot, because of the fact that he liked Mexicanos. And he liked the poor people, too. He made a big stink out of it in the *Houston Press*, where they brought all the city and the county [department] heads and all that together to the county courthouse on Fender Street, that's where we used to hold our meet-ings, we went out there and told them, *How come they didn't hire Mexi-*

cans? They said "[Mexicans] were all too short, they didn't even have no high school education, nothing." We asked them, *What are the qualifications? . . .* "You gotta be 5'10", weigh 165 pounds, be a high school graduate."

So one of the activists—name was Ruben Navarro—said, "All those who meet those qualifications, stand up." About 50 of them stand up there. Police chief didn't say nothing . . . [then] he said, "Well, OK, tomorrow, be at the city hall, 9th floor." I think they hired about 39 of them, 39 of them, all Mexicanos . . . that's how we fought discrimination.[9]

Eguía said there had been no riots or public protests to ensure integration of public safety in Houston, a fact in which he took obvious pride. In Alpine, Pete Gallego Sr., was proud that he and his community had done it on their own, without organizations coming in to advocate and creating greater turbulence. And in San Antonio, Pete Tijerina said he admired the picketers. "My dilemma is that as a person, I'm a coward and do not march. I think of my family and myself first. . . . The Mexicano of the 1970s will have to take a stand or forever hide under the bed."[10] Seen as a simple exercise of First Amendment rights, marches, picket lines, and protest rallies should not inspire fear, but public displays of discontent are regarded as somehow un-American by some Latinos.[11]

These three treatments represent only a small slice of U.S. history. Stories like the first two local ones played out in major cities and small towns across Texas, and indeed, across the Southwest and the Midwest. They are stories of men and women who fervently believed they could transform a system that was built in such a way as to discount their value and curtail their participation. They went about their mission doggedly: in the face of obstacles and setbacks, they forged ahead. Even when they lost personally, they never stopped believing in the righteousness of their cause.

A recurring theme throughout these three pieces is the Mexican American community's insistence on exerting control over itself. In the case of the people in the Alpine schools, Pete Gallego Sr. spoke proudly of his community solving its own problems, firmly insisting on not being part of another organization's larger agenda. The Gallegos and their neighbors did accept intervention by elected officials, but it was the parents' choice, not a decision made externally. In the instance of the integration of El Paso's police and fire departments, it was the Mexican American community's initial insistence on electing a Mexican American mayoral candidate that would open doors. And in 1970, when the Ford Foundation stepped in and told the board of directors it would be required to restructure and relocate to another city, one of the reasons given to avoid moving to Washington, D.C., was that it had been the foundation's suggestion.

In the end, MALDEF board members saved face by deciding to relocate to San Francisco, not Washington. But otherwise, the board conceded to the foundation's demands. It was the only true option to them, the compromise required to change their world.

Notes

INTRODUCTION

1. Jack B. Forbes, *Hearing Before the United States Commission on Civil Rights, San Antonio, Texas, December 9–14, 1968* (Washington, D.C.: Government Printing Office, 1969), 24–36. Forbes compared the Mexican American experience to similar experiences of "border minorities" in Europe. "That is . . . they compare with Hungarians in Roumania [*sic*], with Arabs in Israel, with Greeks in Turkey, and groups of that nature—very, very long term minorities that overlap national boundaries," 25.

2. David J. Weber, *Myth and the History of the Hispanic Southwest: Essays*, 1st ed. (Albuquerque: University of New Mexico Press, 1988), 134.

3. Rodolfo Acuña, *Occupied America: A History of Chicanos*, 7th ed. (Boston: Longman, 2011), 51.

4. David Montejano, *Anglos and Mexicans in the Making of Texas, 1836–1986* (Austin: University of Texas Press, 1987), 311.

5. For anthropologists, this might be termed "internal colonialism," a system in which a group is held in relative powerlessness by the dominant group. Barrera, Muñoz, and Ornelas provide a framework by which to understand what is entailed in internal colonialism. To effect such an imbalance of power, certain mechanisms must be in place, including the following: (1) physical force and other types of repression, sometimes at the hands of law enforcement officials; (2) political disenfranchisement, which may employ tools such as the poll tax or literacy tests; and (3) exclusion from political parties and governmental representation. See Mario Barrera, Carlos Muñoz, and Charles Ornelas, "The Barrio as an Internal Colony," in *La Causa Política: A Chicano Politics Reader*, ed. F. Chris Garcia (Notre Dame, Ind.: University of Notre Dame Press, 1974), 281–301.

6. For a discussion of how some Mexican American elites in the Southwest effected changes, see Richard Griswold del Castillo and Arnoldo De León, *North to Aztlán: A History of Mexican Americans in the United States* (New York: Twayne 1996), 31–33.

7. Julie Leininger Pycior, "La Raza Organizes Mexican American Life in San Antonio, 1915–1930, as Reflected in Mutualista Activities" (PhD diss., University of Notre Dame, 1979), 147.

8. Phillip B. Gonzales, "'La Junta de Indignación': Hispano Repertoire of Collective Protest in New Mexico, 1884–1993," *Western Historical Quarterly* 31, no. 2 (Summer 2000): 161–186.

9. Rodolfo Acuña, *Occupied America*, 119.

10. Richard Griswold del Castillo, "La Raza Hispano Americana: The Emergence of an Urban Culture among the Spanish Speaking of Los Angeles, 1850–1880" (master's thesis, UCLA, 1974), 62–63.

11. Ibid., 147–149.

12. Ibid., 150–151.

13. Ibid.

14. Ibid., 151.

15. Ibid., 152.

16. Pycior, "La Raza Organizes Mexican American Life," 150.

17. Ibid., 97.

18. Cynthia Orozco, *No Mexicans, Women, or Dogs Allowed: The Rise of the Mexican American Civil Rights Movement* (Austin: University of Texas Press, 2009), 69.

19. Ibid.

20. Ibid., 91.

21. Ibid.

22. Ibid., 153. She provided no evidence for the latter claim.

23. José de la Luz Sáenz, *Los México-Americanos en la Gran Guerra* (San Antonio, Tex.: Artes Gráficas, 1933). The diary was translated into English by the University of Texas history professor Emilio Zamora in 2014: *The World War I Diary of José de la Luz Sáenz* (College Station: Texas A&M University Press, 2014).

24. Alonso S. Perales, *En Defensa de mi Raza* (San Antonio, Tex.: Artes Gráficas, 1936–1937).

25. For more on the civil rights activities of the World War I veterans in Texas, see José A. Ramirez, *To the Line of Fire!: Mexican Texans and World War I* (College Station: Texas A&M University Press, 2009), particularly chapter 7, which deals with the veterans' return.

26. Miguel David Tirado, "Mexican American Community Political Organization: 'The Key to Chicano Political Power,'" in *La Causa Política: A Chicano Politics Reader*, ed. F. Chris Garcia (Notre Dame, Ind.: University of Notre Dame Press, 1974).

27. Roybal served on the L.A. City Council for thirteen years. He was later elected to Congress, representing the 25th Congressional District from 1962 to 1993.

28. For more information about the G.I. Forum, see Julie Leininger Pycior, *LBJ and Mexican Americans: The Paradox of Power* (Austin: University of Texas Press, 1997); Henry Ramos, *The American GI Forum: In Pursuit of the Dream, 1948–1983* (Houston: Arte Público, 1998); Vernon Carl Allsup, *The American G.I. Forum: Origins*

and Evolution (monograph, Center for Mexican American Studies, UT-Austin, 1982; distributed by the University of Texas Press).

29. Armando Navarro, *The Cristal Experiment: A Chicano Struggle for Community Control* (Madison: University of Wisconsin Press, 1998), 17–25. See also John Staples Shockley, *Chicano Revolt in a Texas Town* (Notre Dame, Ind.: University of Notre Dame Press, 1974).

30. Ibid., 27.

31. Ibid., 48.

32. According to Navarro, one of the key Raza Unida organizers, José Ángel Gutiérrez, favored the name Mexican American Democratic Party, but state law required the name of political parties not to exceed three words. Gutiérrez "finally acquiesced for strategic reasons," 63. Navarro interviewed Gutiérrez for *The Cristal Experiment.*

33. Carlos Alcalá and Jorge Rangel, "Project Report: De Jure Segregation of Chicanos in Texas Schools," *Harvard Civil Rights-Civil Liberties Review* 7, no. 2 (March 1973): 342. See also chapters in *"Colored Men" and "Hombres Aquí": Hernandez v. Texas and the Emergence of Mexican-American Lawyering*, ed. Michael A. Olivas (Houston: Arte Público, 2006).

34. For more about the inconsistent racial categorizations, see Karl Eschbach and Maggie Rivas-Rodriguez, "Navigating Bureaucratic Imprecision in the Search for an Accurate Count of Latino/a Military Service in WWII," in *U.S. Latina/os and WWII: Mobility, Agency, and Ideology*, ed. Maggie Rivas-Rodriguez and B. O. Olguín (Austin: University of Texas Press, 2014), ix–xix.

35. The "Hispanic" category is not universally embraced by Latinos. Some resist it on the basis that it is a term created by the government, rather than one that originated with the people themselves. Another criticism is that it includes only people of Spanish-speaking backgrounds, leaving out Brazilians. Some prefer the term "Latino," which implies people of Latin American descent but leaves out Spanish Americans.

36. Alfred J. Hernandez, "Civil Service and the Mexican American," *The Mexican American: A New Focus on Opportunity, Testimony Presented at the Cabinet Committee Hearings on Mexican American Affairs* (Inter-Agency Committee on Mexican American Affairs, El Paso, Texas, 26–28, Oct. 1967), 230.

37. Michael A. Olivas, "Review Essay—The Arc of Triumph and the Agony of Defeat: Mexican Americans and the Law," *Journal of Legal Education* 60, no. 2 (Nov. 2010). The University of Houston law professor Michael A. Olivas in 2010 questioned the accuracy of a point made by the New Mexico scholar Cynthia Orozco regarding MALDEF's initial funding. "I do not think that her rendition of the founding of the Mexican American Legal Defense and Educational Fund squares with all the available facts, or that the organization 'contacted Pete Tijerina to use some of . . . [the Ford Foundation] money to help Mexican-American lawyers in Texas with litigation,'" 3. "Remarkably, there has never been a full-length book on MALDEF or its founding, so

the accurate version is still to be told," 362. Here, then, are some of those details, from several sources, that reveal how MALDEF was born.

38. Weber, *Myth and the History of the Hispanic Southwest*. Weber, writing in an essay, "Refighting the Alamo," rejects notions of romanticizing the past. His conclusions (150) about the men who died at the Alamo may also be applied to Mexican American civil rights champions. "It may be that by *manufacturing* heroes from the past we do not necessarily 'uplift and strengthen' the present generation . . . or add to patriotism and pride. Instead, we may only succeed in adding to our self-loathing and cynicism, for as mere human beings we cannot live up to the impossible standards that we set for ourselves when we invent heroes who are larger than life."

39. Ernesto Galarza, *Man of Fire: Selected Writings*, ed. Armando Ibarra and Rodolfo D. Torres (Urbana: University of Illinois Press, 2013).

CHAPTER 1: INTEGRATION *A MORDIDAS* IN ALPINE SCHOOLS

1. Virginia Dominguez, audiotape interview by Maggie Rivas-Rodriguez, Alpine, Texas, August 17, 2012, Voces Oral History Project, Nettie Lee Benson Latin American Collection, University of Texas Libraries.

2. *Alpine Beautiful: The Queen City of West Texas; Health, Wealth, Happiness* (Alpine, Tex.: *Avalanche* Job Office, ca. 1909), 8.

3. Ibid., 1.

4. *Information and History of the Big Bend–Davis Mountains Area: Issued on the Sixtieth Anniversary of the "Avalanche"* (Alpine, Tex.: Webb Pub. Co., 1951), 61.

5. Clifford B. Casey, *Alpine, Texas, Then and Now* (Seagraves, Tex.: Pioneer Book Publishers, 1981), 18.

6. Ibid., 23.

7. Ibid, 21. Forchheimer's was established in 1921 by a New Yorker who had originally emigrated from Germany. It was the department store where both Leyva and Pallanez worked.

8. Ibid., 18.

9. Casey writes that even before Alpine was Murphyville, it was known as Osborne, a name given to a section of the railroad station. Thomas Murphy had registered a plat for the town of Murphyville, Texas, for an area fifty blocks north of the railroad and thirty blocks south of the track. Murphy deeded all streets and alleys to the county, and one block was designated the site of a public school. Railroad officials, perhaps unaware of the shallow water table, negotiated a contract with Murphy to pump water from the Burgess water hole, which he owned. In return, the railroad section station was changed to Murphyville. Later, after Murphy moved to Fort Stockton, residents sought a new name for the station stop (ibid., 18–22).

10. Ibid., 21.

11. Ibid.

12. *Alpine Beautiful*, 5. B. J. Gallego also wrote about Centennial's history: "Nues-

tra Historia," *Alpine Avalanche*, January 15, 2004, A12. Gallego was a teenager on that caravan in 1969.

13. Madero was widely admired for bringing down the dictator Porfirio Diaz in 1910, thus sparking the Mexican Revolution. For more about Madero, see Frank Mc-Lynn, *Villa and Zapata: A History of the Mexican Revolution* (New York: Carroll and Graf, 2000).

14. Information about Clemente J. Uranga is from a videotaped interview with his son, Charles V. Uranga, by Tony Cantú, San Antonio, Texas, January 27, 2001, Voces Oral History Project, Nettie Lee Benson Latin American Collection, University of Texas Libraries.

15. *Information and History of the Big Bend–Davis Mountains Area*, 65.

16. Individuals interviewed in Alpine used those terms to refer to the Catholic school.

17. The photograph was provided by Félix F. Gutiérrez, whose mother was one of the children in the photograph. Gutiérrez's accounts of his grandparents, Febronia and Esau Muñoz, are consistent with obituaries published in the 1967 and 1971 editions of the *Journal of the Southern California-Arizona Annual Conference of the United Methodist Church* (Los Angeles: United Methodist Center, 1967, 1971). Information on the Alpine school, however, was not included in the obituaries.

18. Abelardo Baeza, "La Escuela Escondida: History of the Morgan School in Alpine, Texas, 1929–1954," *Journal of Big Bend Studies* 6 (Jan. 1994): 85.

19. The exact wording in the 1876 Texas Constitution, Article 7, Section 7, is, "Separate schools shall be provided for the white and colored children, and impartial provision shall be made for both," http://tarlton.law.utexas.edu/constitutions/text/IART07.html.

20. "Racial Segregation in Alpine's Public Schools Abolished," *Alpine Avalanche*, July 15, 1955, 1.

21. Abelardo Baeza, "La Escuela del Barrio: A History of the Alpine Centennial School: 1936–1969," *Journal of Big Bend Studies* 4 (Jan. 1992): 4 (reprinted as a monograph, 2004).

22. As noted in the introduction, the flavor of the interviews with men and women in Alpine is retained by including lengthy quotes herein.

23. Mario T. García, *Mexican Americans: Leadership, Ideology, and Identity, 1930–1960* (New Haven, Conn.: Yale University Press, 1989), 7. Interviews with Latinos and Latinas of the World War II generation reveal that the identification as "American" is one that eluded them, even in many cases when returning servicemen were wearing their military uniforms. One man, Armando Flores, whose ancestors were early Spanish settlers of the territory now known as Texas, said he wasn't called an "American" until one of his officers reprimanded him and other servicemen, telling them that "American soldiers stand at attention, on a cold day or a hot day; they never keep their hands in their pockets." Flores said: "The funny thing about it, and the reason that I remember that was because nobody had ever called me an American until that time. I had been called a lot of things . . . [like] wetback and spic, and greaser.

. . . That was the first time in my life that I had been called an American." Armando Flores, videotape interview by Bettina Luis, Corpus Christi, Texas, March 24, 2001, Voces Oral History Project, Nettie Lee Benson Latin American Collection, University of Texas Libraries.

24. U.S. Commission on Civil Rights, *Stranger in One's Land*, Clearinghouse Publication no. 19 (Washington, D.C.: Government Printing Office, May 1970), 25.

25. Guadalupe San Miguel Jr., *"Let All of Them Take Heed": Mexican Americans and the Campaign for Educational Equality in Texas, 1910–1981* (Austin: University of Texas Press, 1987), 33.

26. Carlos Kevin Blanton, *The Strange Career of Bilingual Education in Texas, 1836–1981* (College Station: Texas A&M University Press, 2004), 76. There were earlier laws passed as well, but they lacked enforcement power.

27. Ibid.

28. Virginia Dominguez, audiotape interview by Maggie Rivas-Rodriguez, Alpine, Texas, August 17, 2012, Voces Oral History Project, Nettie Lee Benson Latin American Collection, University of Texas Libraries.

29. Leo Dominguez, audiotape interview by Maggie Rivas-Rodriguez, Alpine, Texas, August 17, 2012, Voces Oral History Project, Nettie Lee Benson Latin American Collection, University of Texas Libraries.

30. Interestingly, her husband, Francisco, was very active in the integration movement and was one of the people on the caravan trip. She remembered very little about his involvement when she was interviewed in 2012. But former Alpine school board member Pete A. Gallego Sr. described Francisco Valenzuela as very committed to the cause.

31. Mary Pallanez, audiotape interview, Alpine, Texas, Aug. 17, 2012, Voces Oral History Project, Nettie Lee Benson Latin American Collection, University of Texas Libraries.

32. Elidia Leyva, audiotape interview, Alpine, Texas, Aug. 17, 2012, Voces Oral History Project, Nettie Lee Benson Latin American Collection, University of Texas Libraries.

33. B. J. Gallego, "Nuestra Historia," *Alpine Avalanche*, January 15, 2004, 12. The photographs are included in wall display cases at the Centennial building, which now houses state government offices.

34. Leyva, interview.

35. Ibid.

36. United States Commission on Civil Rights, *Hearing before the United States Commission on Civil Rights: Hearing Held in San Antonio, Texas, December 9–14, 1968* (Washington, D.C.: Government Printing Office, 1969), 766.

37. United States Commission on Civil Rights, *Stranger in One's Land*, Clearinghouse Publication no. 19 (Washington, D.C.: Government Printing Office, May 1970), 23.

38. *Mendez v. Westminster School District of Orange County*, 64 F. Supp. 544 (D.C. Cal. 1946), aff'd 161 F.2d 774 (9th Cir. 1947).

39. Philippa Strum, Mendez v. Westminster: *School Desegregation and Mexican-American Rights* (Lawrence: University Press of Kansas, 2010).

40. San Miguel, 119.

41. Texas Attorney General's Office, *Digest of Opinions of the Attorney General of Texas, 1947–1981* (Austin: Texas Attorney General's Office, 1942–1982), 39.

42. J. W. Edgar to County Superintendents of Schools and Presidents of Boards of Trustees, June, 21, 1950, J. W. Edgar Records, Box 24, Segregation Letters Folder, Accession no. 178-174. Record Group 701-1978/174, Texas State Archives.

43. G.I. Forum, *News Bulletin* 1, no. 4 (Dec. 15, 1952): 3, G.I. Forum Papers, Nettie Lee Benson Latin American Collection, University of Texas Libraries.

44. G. M. Blackman to Hector P. Garcia, August 22, 1952, J. W. Edgar Records, Box 24, Segregation Letters Folder, Accession no. 178-174. Record Group 701-1978/174, Texas State Archives.

45. F. M. Glaze to J. W. Edgar, August 4, 1950, J. W. Edgar Records, Box 16, Segregation Letters Folder, Record Group 701-1978/174, Texas State Archives.

46. J. W. Edgar to F. M. Glaze, August 16, 1950, ibid.

47. G.I. Forum, *News Bulletin* 3, no. 8 (April 1955): 1, 4, J. W. Edgar Records, Texas State Archives.

48. Ibid.

49. Carlos Alcalá and Jorge Rangel, "Project Report: De Jure Segregation of Chicanos in Texas Schools," *Harvard Civil Rights-Civil Liberties Review* 7, no. 2 (March 1973). The deposed Superintendent Woods, who had been sympathetic to the case of Mexican American desegregation, was instructed to serve in an advisory position to the new commissioner. At the end of his term of office, both the advisory position and the superintendent position were eliminated.

50. Ibid., 339.

51. *Delgado v. Bastrop Independent School District* (1948), Civil Action No. 333, District Court of the United States, Western District of Texas.

52. *Digest of Opinions of the Attorney General of Texas*, 39. In 1961, when this writer was being registered for first grade in a small South Texas town, the registrar, who was also a school principal, first placed her in such a segregated class—even though English was her primary language and her mother, who accompanied her, spoke flawless English. There was no test administered before determining that she would be in the segregated class. This is only anecdotal evidence; there appears to be only similar anecdotal evidence on this matter.

53. Guadalupe San Miguel Jr., "The Struggle against Separate and Unequal Schools: Middle Class Mexican Americans and the Desegregation Campaign in Texas, 1929–1957," *History of Education Quarterly* 23, no. 3 (1983): 350.

54. Joe R. Humphrey J. W. Edgar, Sept. 29, 1954, J. W. Edgar Records, Texas Education Agency, Box 22, Segregation and Latin American Folder, Accession no. 174, Record Group 701-1978/174.

55. *The Wildcat*, Carrizo Springs High School Annual Yearbook, 1957. Accessed at the Dimmit County Public Library.

56. During World War II, as American men entered the military and more American women took high-paying defense contractor jobs, as well as other jobs for the displaced men, the U.S. government sought to import Mexican laborers for work, mainly in agriculture and railroads. Because Texas had such a poor record for treatment of Mexicans, the Mexican government refused to allow braceros into the state until 1947. By contrast, other employers in other states were able to get braceros in 1942. See Emilio Zamora, "Mexico's Wartime Intervention on Behalf of Mexicans in the United States," in *Mexican Americans and World War II*, ed. Maggie Rivas-Rodriguez (Austin: University of Texas Press, 2004), 230–232. Zamora offers a concise explanation of the grievances of the Mexican government and how it used those to leverage better treatment of its citizens by Texas employers.

57. "First Commissioner of Education Faced with Challenging Responsibilities," in *Weekly Report to Members of the Good Neighbor Commission* 1, no. 10 (October 13, 1950), J. W. Edgar Records, Texas State Archives.

58. Ibid., 24.

59. Henry Leblanc to J. W. Edgar, Aug. 13, 1952, J. W. Edgar Records, Box 16, Segregation Letters Folder, Record Group 701-1978/174, Texas Education Agency Collection.

60. J. W. Edgar to Henry Leblanc, Aug. 28, 1942, J. W. Edgar Records, Texas Education Agency Collection.

61. Mrs. W. C. Rich to J. W. Edgar, May 15, 1955, J. W. Edgar Records, Box 22, Segregation-Latin Americans Folder, Accession no. 174, Record Group 701-1978/174, Texas Education Agency Collection.

62. J. W. Edgar to Mrs. W. C. Rich, May 30, 1955, J. W. Edgar Records, Texas Education Agency Collection.

63. See the introduction to this volume.

64. David Montejano, *Anglos and Mexicans in the Making of Texas, 1836–1986* (Austin: University of Texas Press, 1987), 262–263.

65. In *Kilgarlin v. Martin* the Supreme Court ruled that Texas's system of apportioning state legislative seats by land mass rather than population was unconstitutional. Mary Ellen Curtin, in "Reaching for Power: Barbara C. Jordan and Liberals in the Texas Legislature, 1966–1972," *Southwestern Historical Quarterly* 108, no. 2 (Oct. 2004): 210–231, writes that "altogether liberals gained five seats in the 1966 Senate race. As the *Houston Chronicle* noted, 'it is significant that Tuesday's election put into office twelve senators generally regarded as conservative, twelve expected usually to line up as liberals and seven best described as moderates.' Besides [Barbara] Jordan, the Senate contained Democratic liberals such as labor lawyer Oscar Mauzy from Dallas, 'Babe' Schwartz from Galveston, and Joseph Bernal from San Antonio. Although certainly not radicals or militants, these men had liberal proposals that ranged from introducing a corporate income tax and implementing a state board for regulating telephone service to establishing a minimum wage. These were not far-fetched goals: with eleven votes liberals could block legislation introduced by the majority or trade support for other measures to get some legislation accomplished" (219).

66. Alberto Rojo, audiotape interview by Maggie Rivas-Rodriguez, Alpine, Texas, July 8, 2013, Voces Oral History Project, Nettie Lee Benson Latin American Collection, University of Texas Libraries.

67. There was some integration at the lower levels—there was only one band, for instance.

68. Pete A. Gallego Sr., videotape interview by Maggie Rivas-Rodriguez, El Paso, Texas, March 9, 2001, Voces Oral History Project, Nettie Lee Benson Latin American Collection, University of Texas Libraries.

69. Ibid.

70. Ibid.

71. "School Meet Set Tonight," *Alpine Avalanche*, March 27, 1969, 1.

72. Ibid.

73. "Bids Asked on Central Classrooms," *Alpine Avalanche*, May 15, 1969, 1.

74. "Central School Faces Big Fall Enrollment," *Alpine Avalanche*, May 15, 1969, 1.

75. Ibid.

76. "'Open Campus' Rule Continued," *Alpine Avalanche*, July 10, 1969, 1.

77. "Mexican-Americans Ask Integration of Schools," *Alpine Avalanche*, July 24, 1969, 16.

78. When the group returned home, and Sotelo's statement was repeated, others were angry at him, Leyva said. It appeared that he was equivocating on the matter of segregation.

79. "Alpine School Discrimination Charge Is Aired," *Alpine Avalanche*, July 31, 1969, 1.

80. "Legislators Favor Alpine School Plan," *San Antonio Express*, August 12, 1969, 11A.

81. Ibid.

82. Elena Gallego, speaking on Pete Gallego's interview by Maggie Rivas-Rodriguez.

83. The motion was made by Harvey Gilliam and seconded by Pete Gallego.

84. "Central, Centennial Plants to be Used," *Alpine Avalanche*, August 21, 1969, 1. Only one board member refused to sign on to the consolidation. Trustee Thad Corkins said he had spoken to TEA official J. A. Anderson and that Anderson advocated split sessions, with all grades held at Central in two sessions: some students would attend in the morning and others in the afternoon. But the problems with that proposal were numerous: working parents would be disadvantaged, the logistics of administering it would be difficult, and the school day would be two hours shorter, which would possibly not pass approval by the Texas Education Agency.

85. Rojo, interview.

86. "Parents Air Complaints," *Alpine Avalanche*, September 4, 1969, 1.

CHAPTER 2: THE MULTISTEP INTEGRATION
OF THE EL PASO POLICE DEPARTMENT

1. The minutes of the regular El Paso City Council meeting of April 14, 1960, show that Armendariz was appointed to fill the seat of Andy Fuentes on the Civil Service Commission.

2. Albert Armendariz, videotape interview by Maggie Rivas-Rodriguez, El Paso, Texas, March 10, 2001, Voces Oral History Project, Nettie Lee Benson Latin American Collection, University of Texas Libraries.

3. Leon Eguía, videotape interview by Liliana Velasquez, Houston, Texas, March 2, 2002, Voces Oral History Project, Nettie Lee Benson Latin American Collection, University of Texas Libraries. Eguía said in the interview that Houston began pushing for change in 1953, when he was the president of LULAC Council 60. "At that time, we had an activist [who] . . . was a writer for the *Houston Press* . . . name of Sandy Anderson, and he helped us a lot, because of the fact that he liked Mexicanos. And he liked the poor people, too. He made a big stink out of it in the *Houston Press*, where they brought all the city and the county [department] heads and all that together to the county courthouse on Fender Street, . . . where we used to hold our meetings; we went out there and [asked] them: *How come [you don't] hire Mexicans?* They said [Mexicans] were all too short, they didn't even have no high school education, nothing. We asked them: *What are the qualifications?* 'You gotta be 5′10″, weigh 165 pounds, be a high school graduate.'

"So one of the activists—name was Ruben Navarro—said, 'All those who meet those qualifications, stand up.' About 50 of them stand up there. Police chief didn't say nothing . . . [then] he said, 'Well, OK, tomorrow, be at the city hall, 9th floor,' I think they hired about 39 of them, 39 of them, all Mexicanos . . . that's how we fought discrimination." In 1956, Eguía joined the fire department, the eighth Mexican American to do so—he and his fellow Mexican Americans kept count. Before Eguía joined, there were so few Mexican American firefighters that that you could count them on one hand. But one who joined in 1951 was Mario Gallegos. Gallegos provides a detailed account of the early days in the department, when his Spanish-speaking skills were required to serve Houston residents. He also says that he helped recruit and prepare other Mexican American applicants. Once exams began determining promotions, there was further advancement. See Mario Gallegos, "History of Hispanic Firefighters in Houston," in *Hispanics in Houston and Harris County, 1519–1986: A Sesquicentennial Celebration*, ed. Dorothy F. Caram, Anthony G. Dworkin, and Néstor Rodríguez (Houston: Houston Hispanic Forum, 1989), 192–194.

4. Maggie Rivas, "Brothers in Arms," *Dallas Life Magazine*, December 6, 1992, 14.

5. Oscar J. Martinez, *The Chicanos of El Paso: An Assessment of Progress* (El Paso: Texas Western Press, 1980), 6.

6. W. H. Timmons, *El Paso: A Borderlands History* (El Paso: Texas Western Press, 1990). Timmons offers a detailed account of precolonial times to the late 1970s.

7. Mario T. García, *Desert Immigrants: The Mexicans of El Paso, 1880–1920* (New

Haven, Conn.: Yale University Press, 1981). See especially the introduction and chapter 1, in which Garcia outlines the effects of Diaz's land policies on the rural populations in Mexico. García (35) notes that it is difficult to arrive at firm figures for the number of El Paso's Mexican immigrants between 1880 and 1920 because immigration authorities did not maintain good records, and because of the seasonal movement across the border for employment reasons. He also notes that there were several unguarded crossing points that immigrants could access without notice.

8. Mario T. García, *The Making of a Mexican American Mayor: Raymond L. Telles of El Paso* (El Paso: Texas Western Press, 1998). García (163) writes of Mexicans attending large dances the night before an election and finding, on election morning, that they were locked in until the polls opened and they had been transported to local precincts to cast their votes. García (165–171) explains that these types of tactics were practiced in other areas as well: Mexican American voters were delivered in exchange for parties, beer, and cash payments.

9. Ibid., 171.

10. Ibid., 19.

11. Rudolph O. de la Garza, "Voting Patterns in 'Bi-Cultural El Paso': a Contextual Analysis of Chicano Voting Behavior," *Aztlán: A Journal of Chicano Studies* 5, nos. 1–2 (1974): 239.

12. Texas Advisory Committee to the U.S. Commission on Civil Rights, *Texas: The State of Civil Rights, Ten Years Later, 1968–1978* (Washington, D.C.: Government Printing Office, 1980), 45.

13. Mexican-American Legal Defense and Education Fund, "Draft Proposal to the Ford Foundation," August 7, 1967, 13, MALDEF Records, PA 06800248, Ford Foundation Archives.

14. Raymond Telles, typescript of interview by Oscar J. Martinez, Interview no. 182, October 22, 1975, Institute of Oral History, University of Texas at El Paso.

15. These points have come up repeatedly in interviews for the Voces Oral History Project. Several veterans have said that they had never before believed they were capable of the high-level accomplishments they achieved in the military.

16. Jay Teachman and Vaughn R. A. Call, "The Effect of Military Service on Education, Occupational & Income Attainment," *Social Science Research* 25 (1966): 5.

17. There are numerous examples of this. See for example the case of Felix Longoria, who was killed in battle in the Pacific in the closing days of World War II. In 1949, his remains were being exhumed and shipped to his hometown of Three Rivers, Texas. His widow, however, was told by the local funeral home director that she could not hold his wake at the funeral parlor because the "white people wouldn't like it." The Felix Longoria story became national news, in which the national news media framed it as an example of an American hero who had died in service to his country yet would not receive equal treatment because of his ethnicity. The definitive book of the case is Patrick James Carroll, *Felix Longoria's Wake: Bereavement, Racism, and the Rise of Mexican American Activism* (Austin: University of Texas Press, 2003).

18. See Philip E. Converse and Georges Dupeux, "De Gaulle and Eisenhower: The

Public Image of the Victorious General," in Angus Campbell et al., *Elections and the Political Order* (New York: Wiley, 1966). Converse and Dupeux outline how de Gaulle and Eisenhower, both generals during World War II, were able to leverage their wartime accomplishments to become postwar leaders of their respective countries. "The military hero is not revered specifically for his military contributions to society, nor is he praised for his military virtues. He is rather seen as a man of integrity and sincerity" (344).

19. Maggie Rivas, "Brothers in Arms," *Dallas Life Magazine*, December 6, 1992, 14.

20. It could be said that Telles was, by nature, cautious in taking on greater roles. For instance, when it came time to decide whether to run for mayor, he was again prodded. And in 1961, when President John F. Kennedy asked him to be ambassador to Costa Rica, again he was reluctant.

21. Telles would later say he didn't know why the county clerk's office was targeted for his first attempt to win a public seat.

22. The poll tax was outlawed in federal elections by the 1964 passage of the Twenty-Fourth Amendment, signed by President Lyndon B. Johnson. Two years later, the U.S. Supreme Court extended the ban of poll taxes to state elections in *Harper v. Virginia Board of Elections*.

23. Raymond Telles, typescript of inteview by Oscar J. Martinez. Martinez pressed Telles about how the Mexican Americans viewed the poll tax. *Was it seen as being a form of discrimination, a way to prevent greater electoral participation?* Telles responded that he never heard people putting it that way, that since all voters were required to pay the $1.75, it seemed "normal." Others saw the poll tax as a deliberate effort to disenfranchise African American, Mexican American, and low-income voters. And in fact, it was later eliminated at both the federal and state levels as an unwarranted deterrent to participating in electoral decision-making.

24. García, *Making of a Mexican American Mayor*, 37.

25. Ibid., 38.

26. Ibid., 40.

27. Ibid., 42.

28. García (ibid., 43) writes that Telles's office reported net earnings for the previous three years as $87,147; his predecessor's earned only $30,439 in eleven years. He was recalled into active duty in early 1942 and returned in September 1952. While he was away, his wife, Delfina, took over his country clerk duties on an unpaid basis.

29. Albert Armendariz, audiotape interview by Mario T. García, El Paso, Texas, October 26, 1982, in author's possession.

30. García, *The Making of a Mexican American Mayor*, 58.

31. William V. D'Antonio and William H. Form, *Influentials in Two Border Cities: A Study in Community Decision-Making* (Notre Dame, Ind.: University of Notre Dame Press, 1965), 231.

32. Ibid, 91.

33. Ibid, 99.

34. Ibid., 98.

35. Ibid., 100.

36. Ibid., 101.

37. Albert Armendariz, videotape interview by Maggie Rivas-Rodriguez, El Paso, Texas, March 16, 2001, Voces Oral History Project, Nettie Lee Benson Latin American Collection, University of Texas Libraries.

38. Ibid.

39. Minutes, Regular El Paso City Council Meeting, April 14, 1960. At this meeting, the El Paso City Council accepted the resignation of Andy Fuentes and approved the appointment of Albert Armendariz to fill Fuentes's unexpired term. The city council meeting minutes for November 8, 1962, show that Armendariz's appointment was extended through November 8, 1964. According to the records of the Civil Service Commission, Armendariz was appointed to the chair in 1960 and 1962. In 1963, the method for selecting the chairman was changed to one based on an election by the commissioners. In the July 24, 1963, meeting, the commissioners thanked Armendariz for his service and elected James Malone chair (El Paso Civil Service Commission minutes of a special meeting, July 24, 1963). Armendariz was not the first Mexican American to serve on the commission. City council and Civil Service Commission records indicate there were at least two other Mexican Americans who preceded Armendariz: Andy Fuentes (whose unexpired term Armendariz filled) and Gabrielle Navarette. It is not known how either Fuentes or Navarette viewed the performance of Mexican Americans vis-à-vis Mexican Americans.

40. This is reflected in the city commissioners' meeting minutes for the time that Armendariz was on the board.

41. In *Desert Immigrants* (169), García writes of a Círculo de Amigos in the early 1900s, a circle of friends made up of maintenance workers, "shovel men," and garbage collectors.

42. Armendariz, audiotape interview with Mario T. García, El Paso, Texas, Oct. 26, 1983, in author's possession.

43. Ari Hoogenboom, "The Pendleton Act and the Civil Service," *The American Historical Review* 64, no. 2 (Jan. 1959). Hoogenboom (302) writes that the job system provided a payroll so elected officials could pay a staff of what would be known today as "political hacks" and ward heelers. This system was also a primary source of that important commodity with which elections are won—money. Local, state, and federal politicians might assess a civil servant yearly fee that ranged from 2 to 7 percent of the employee's annual salary.

44. Sean M. Theriault, "Patronage, the Pendleton Act, and the Power of the People," *Journal of Politics* 65, no. 1 (Feb. 2003): 52.

45. Ibid., 56.

46. Theriault also notes that the Pendleton Act prohibited mandatory campaign contributions, so-called political assessments. One scholar, Louise Overacker, found that those "political assessments" made up as much as three-quarters of all campaign contributions after the Reconstruction era. Louise Overacker, *Money in Elections* (New

York: Macmillan, 1932). Theriault ("Patronage," 52) writes that the Pendleton Act also called for entrance exams for would-be bureaucrats. These exams replaced loyalty with merit as the medium of exchange in securing political appointments. Up until the exams were in place, in a complicit agreement with the president and in conjunction with the local party elites, members could make political appointments. These two mandates were among the early steps that politicians wrested from the strong political cal parties that dominated the nineteenth-century Congress. Political employees were still appointed, but they lacked the job security of falling under the "classified system."

47. African Americans had found employment opportunities with the U.S. Postal Service since almost the start of the agency. See Philip F. Rubio in *There's Always Work at the Post Office* (Chapel Hill: University of North Carolina Press, 2010).

48. Ibid., 4. Rubio has a full three pages (2–4) listing African Americans who either worked in the post office or whose parents or grandparents did. Among them were the actor Danny Glover's parents; the historian John Hope Franklin's attorney father; and the comedian and social critic Dick Gregory, who had a day job at the Chicago post office.

49. There is anecdotal evidence here. Armando Vasquez, of Marfa, tells of his family operating a combination post office and grocery store in the settlement of Casa Piedras, near Marfa. Armando Vasquez, videotape interview by Maggie Rivas-Rodriguez, Marfa, Texas, August 17, 2012, Voces Oral History Project, Nettie Lee Benson Latin American Collection, University of Texas Libraries.

50. Consider, for example, the story of Mike Aguirre. Aguirre, a World War II U.S. Army and later Merchant Marine veteran, moved to San Marcos, Texas, and took the exams for letter carrier, but he was turned down. He heard, "through the grapevine," that he had scored better than Anglos who were hired, and he complained to Senator Ralph Yarbrough. Aguirre was soon hired, becoming, he said, San Marcos's first Hispanic letter carrier. Mike Aguirre, videotape interview by Aryn Sedler, San Marcos, Texas, March 24, 2000, Voces Oral History Project, Nettie Lee Benson Latin American Collection, University of Texas Libraries.

51. Hernandez was also a World War II veteran, having served in the army in Europe and Africa during the war. When he returned to his hometown of Houston, he was deeply troubled by the pervasive discrimination. He was determined to move out of the state—either to Mexico or up north—where he and his family would be treated better. But his wife, Herminia Casas Hernandez, counseled him to stay and work to improve conditions for Mexican Americans in Texas. Hernandez went to law school and made civil rights his life's work. Alfred J. Hernandez, videotape interview by Ernest Eguía, Houston, Texas, October 24, 2002, Voces Oral History Project, Nettie Lee Benson Latin American Collection, University of Texas Libraries.

52. Alfred J. Hernandez, "Civil Service and the Mexican American," *The Mexican American: A New Focus on Opportunity, Testimony Presented at the Cabinet Committee Hearings on Mexican American Affairs* (Inter-Agency Committee on Mexican American Affairs, El Paso, Texas, Oct. 26–28, 1967), 230.

53. Ibid.

54. Ibid.

55. Ibid., 227.

56. Ibid.

57. Ibid., 232.

58. It has been demonstrated time and again, after a courtroom victory, or after a law was passed, opponents found resourceful ways to prevent enactment. See Paul Burstein, *Discrimination, Jobs, and Politics: The Struggle for Equal Employment Opportunity in the United States Since the New Deal* (Chicago: University of Chicago Press, 1985), 4. In writing about the passage and implications of the Equal Employment Opportunity legislation, Burstein says that supporters "clearly believed that the democratic political process may be used to change the formal and informal rules by which jobs and incomes are allocated in a society—to change how employers decide whom to hire and promote, how unions decide whom to admit into membership, and how, in general, people are treated in the labor market." Others, however, are skeptical. "In this view, laws purporting to produce economic or social change by direct action will be suppressed," Burstein writes (4).

59. For analyses of different racial attitudes toward government intervention in federal employment, see: Ronald T. Takaki, *Iron Cages: Race and Culture in Nineteenth-Century America* (New York: Knopf, distributed by Random House, 1979). Pages 13–16, in particular, address the issue. For instance, although 64 percent of whites felt that blacks should have the same opportunities for federal jobs, only 43 percent believed the government should act to ensure that equality of opportunity.

60. Armendariz, interview. In fact, Freddy Bonilla, who joined the El Paso Police Department in 1959, said he spent one year as a downtown patrolman and then ten years as a motorcycle patrolman. Freddy Bonilla, audiotape interview by Maggie Rivas-Rodriguez, El Paso, Texas, August, 11, 2011, Voces Oral History Project, Nettie Lee Benson Latin American Collection, University of Texas Libraries.

61. Armendariz, interview.

62. Minutes, Regular Meeting of the El Paso Civil Service Commission, May 16, 1963, 3.

63. García, *The Making of a Mexican American Mayor*, 121. Telles had been a stalwart campaigner for Kennedy and had campaigned for him in California with Sen. Dennis Chavez (D-NM). After Kennedy was elected, it was widely speculated that Telles might be offered a post in the Kennedy administration.

64. García, *The Making of a Mexican American Mayor*, 125.

65. Ibid., 133–140.

66. Ibid. García (147) writes that White took all twelve counties in the 16th Congressional District with 40,147 votes to Telles's 20,016.

67. See for example Oscar J. Martinez, *The Chicanos of El Paso: An Assessment of Progress* (El Paso: Texas Western Press, 1980). See also William V. D'Antonio and William H. Form, *Influentials in Two Border Cities: A Study in Community Decision-Making* (Notre Dame, Ind.: University of Notre Dame Press, 1965). García, in *The Making of a Mexican American Mayor*, also addresses this point.

68. El Paso Police Department 2012 Annual Report, 17. Available at http://home
.elpasotexas.gov/police-department/annual-report.php/. El Paso Fire Department
2012 Annual Report, 36. Available at http://home.elpasotexas.gov/fire-department
/_documents/2012ANNUALREPORT.pdf/.

CHAPTER 3: MALDEF: BORN INTO THE CROSSWINDS
OF THE CHICANO MOVEMENT

1. It had first been established by the U.S. Supreme Court in 1880, after Reconstruction, that African American (males) should not be excluded from juries. In the
case of *Strauder v. West Virginia*, a black man convicted of murder in West Virginia
challenged the state law that limited jury service to whites. The Supreme Court, citing
the then recently passed Fourteenth Amendment, supported the contention that state
laws should offer equal protection to all, including in the case of jury service. See
Benno C. Schmidt Jr., "Juries, Jurisdiction, and Race Discrimination: The Lost Promise of *Strauder v. West Virginia*," *Texas Law Review* 61, no. 8. And the issue of jury
selection as it affected Mexican Americans was at the heart of the 1954 landmark *Hernandez v. Texas*, discussed in the introduction to this volume. But the issue of discrimination in jury selection continues to be argued to the time of this writing, in some
cases involving gays and lesbians.

2. Steven Harmon Wilson, "Some Are Born White, Some Achieve Whiteness,
and Some Have Whiteness Thrust upon Them: Mexican Americans and the Politics
of Racial Classification in the Federal Judicial Bureaucracy, Twenty-Five Years after
Hernandez v. Texas," in *"Colored Men" and "Hombres Aquí"*: Hernández v. Texas *and
the Emergence of Mexican-American Lawyering*, ed. Michael A. Olivas (Houston: Arte
Público, 2006).

3. Pete Tijerina, videotape interview by Maggie Rivas-Rodriguez, San Antonio,
Texas, October 20, 2002, Voces Oral History Project, Nettie Lee Benson Latin American Collection, University of Texas Libraries.

4. Ibid.

5. James DeAnda, "Civil Rights—Need for Executive Branch to Take Positive
Steps to Rectify Discrimination in Jury Selection, Voting Eligibility and School Enrollment," in *The Mexican American, A New Focus on Opportunity. Testimony Presented at
the Cabinet Committee Hearings on Mexican American Affairs (El Paso, Tex., October
26–28, 1967)*, ed. Inter-Agency Committee on Mexican American Affairs (Washington,
D.C.: Government Printing Office, 1968), 218.

6. Michael D. Davis and Hunter R. Clark, *Thurgood Marshall: Warrior at the Bar,
Rebel on the Bench* (New York: Carol Publishing Group, 1992). Davis and Clark (214)
write that Marshall was suspicious of Martin Luther King at the time that the Southern Leadership Council was using public protests to battle inequality. In remarks to
his legal colleagues, Marshall referred to King as an "opportunist," a "first-rate rabble-
rouser," and a "coward."

7. For more on those earlier organizations, see the introduction to this book.

8. Ibid.

9. For an analysis of the times and the cleavages specifically in San Antonio, birthplace of MALDEF, see David Montejano, *Quixote's Soldiers: A Local History of the Chicano Movement, 1966–1981* (Austin: University of Texas Press, 2010).

10. Leo Cardenas, "MALDF Makes Legal Fight for Chicanos' Rights," *San Antonio Express*, April 17, 1969, 4.

11. José Ángel Gutiérrez, *El Politico: The Mexican American Elected Official* (El Paso: El Dorado, 1972), 27. In this slim volume, Gutiérrez (26) surveyed public officials in Texas and noted that only 32 percent of the officials who responded to the questionnaire considered "protests, marches, or demonstrations as effective methods for the Mexican American to obtain justice." Those respondents most often offered the names of Gonzalez and Peña as effective political leaders.

12. Henry B. Gonzalez to the *San Antonio Express-News*," July 16, 1991, Henry B. Gonzalez papers, Box 2004-127/327, Personal Correspondence, Dolph Briscoe Center for American History, University of Texas at Austin. Gonzalez corrects a news article by, among other things, clarifying that Peña was never his campaign manager.

13. David Montejano, *Anglos and Mexicans in the Making of Texas, 1836–1986* (Austin: University of Texas Press, 1987). Montejano notes that in the 1930s, most urban areas of Texas had hard divisions between Mexican Americans and Anglos, with Mexican Americans at the lower rungs of society. But, he says (254), the border cities of El Paso, Laredo, and Brownsville were exceptions, "where ethnic relations were flexible and pragmatic, that is, more a matter of class than of race."

14. Tijerina, interview.

15. Ibid.

16. Irving Stone, *Clarence Darrow for the Defense: A Biography* (Garden City, N.Y.: Doubleday, Doran, 1941).

17. Tijerina, interview.

18. Jack Greenberg, *Crusaders in the Courts: How a Dedicated Band of Lawyers Fought for the Civil Rights Revolution* (New York: Basic Books, 1994), 46.

19. Ibid.

20. Ibid., 48.

21. All the military branches set up officer-training programs during WWII. The navy's V-12 program provided up to two years of college to their participants, which included students in its college reserve programs. After the college coursework, the men were sent for further officer training. During the time of the V-12 program's existence (July 1, 1943, to June 30, 1946), more than 125,000 men were enrolled at 131 U.S. colleges and universities. See James G. Schneider, *The Navy V12 Program: Leadership for a Lifetime* (Boston: Houghton Mifflin Company, 1987), 45–46.

22. Greenberg, *Crusaders in the Courts*, 50.

23. Ibid., 44. Greenberg writes that "the first postwar classes went to law school through the summers," thus explaining the October graduation.

24. Rawn James Jr., *Root and Branch: Charles Hamilton Houston, Thurgood Mar-*

shall, and the Struggle to End Segregation (New York: Bloomsbury, 2010), 154–155. The National Association for the Advancement of Colored People was established in 1909, in Springfield, Missouri, in direct response to a lynching. Its goal was to ensure "equal rights and opportunities for all." In 1940, the NAACP created a nonprofit organization, the NAACP Legal Defense and Educational Fund, taking advantage of a new tax code that would give deductions to donors who wished to support civil rights efforts that did not involve lobbying and propaganda. In his book *Crusaders in the Courtroom*, Greenberg wrote that "Thurgood Marshall drafted the corporate charter on a yellow pad with his own hand" (19). The NAACP Legal Defense and Educational Fund is known by several names. Some refer to it as the LDF; others know it as the "Inc. Fund"; and some, such as the historian John Hope Franklin, who wrote the forward to Greenberg's book about the Legal Defense Fund, call it the "Ink Fund."

25. Greenberg asserts that in speaking to high school and college students, he never has to explain the case: "It is described in high school social studies texts and has been the subject of at least two documentaries" (*Crusaders in the Courtroom*, 116). He writes that by early 1961, people were speculating that President John F. Kennedy would be appointing a black to a federal court. Thurgood Marshall's name was bandied about, and he had spoken to people in the Kennedy administration, making it clear that he was "only interested in the court of appeals" (ibid., 293–294). Marshall was that year nominated to the U.S. Court of Appeals for the Second Circuit.

26. Thurgood Marshall was nominated to the U.S. Supreme Court by President Lyndon B. Johnson in 1967 and went on to become the first black member of the court that fall. Greenberg has noted how his own race was regarded in relation to his appointment as the LDF's general counsel, offering that Marshall cleared the way for him. Marshall spoke privately to board members, to black newspaper editors, extolling Greenberg's strengths and how race should not be a factor. The day after he was confirmed as general counsel, Greenberg was disappointed by this headline in the *New York Times*: "N.A.A.C.P. Names a White Counsel." Of it, he said (27),"Rather than highlighting the fact that I had been one of Thurgood's senior assistants for several years and had a long history with LDF programs and cases, the *Times* chose to focus on the least relevant aspect of my persona. Of course, the headline was also inaccurate, for though we had gone through great lengths to make clear our separate identity from the NAACP for many years, here was one more indication that the distinction would remain too subtle for some to handle."

27. Greenberg, *Crusaders in the Courts*, 46–49.

28. Sanchez had written to the San Antonio attorney Carlos Cadena fourteen years earlier, saying he had secured funding from the Marshall Trust to begin a test case on "the jury service case"; see George I. Sanchez to Carlos Cadena, Austin, Texas, Oct. 2, 1953. George I. Sanchez Papers, Box 9, Folder 2, Nettie Lee Benson Latin American Collection, University of Texas Libraries. Sanchez had written to Cadena saying that he had received a grant from the Marshall Trust to work on.

29. Pete Tijerina to George I. Sanchez, Austin, Texas, Feb. 22, 1967, George I.

Sanchez Papers, Box 25, Folder 1, Nettie Lee Benson Latin American Collection, University of Texas Libraries.

30. George I. Sanchez to Pete Tijerina, Austin, Texas, Feb. 28, 1967, George I. Sanchez Papers, Box 25, Folder 1. The issue of black-brown rivalry is one that has received some scholarly attention, with a few attributing the Mexican American reluctance to link arms with African Americans to racism. Another view is that Mexican Americans seemed to get ignored in the black-white binary and wished to assert their own identity—and claim full benefits. Evidence of that view abounds. Among Sanchez's papers, there is a letter—dated May 16, 1946, from him to the labor economist and activist Ernesto Galarza—that indicates the two had been involved in the American Council on Race Relations but were withdrawing. "I, too, think that they should either begin doing more to help other racial or cultural groups or else frankly admit that their concern is for the Negro. A clarification of this matter would be very helpful to many of us who, though interested in the Negro, are specializing on some other group." George I. Sanchez Papers, Box 16, Folder 13.

31. Jack Greenberg to Pete Tijerina, January 23, 1967, Henry B. Gonzalez Papers, Box 127/91, Legislative Correspondence, Mexican American Issues, 1967, Dolph Briscoe Center for American History, University of Texas at Austin. In this letter, Greenberg says the LDF is "quite anxious to extend its services to Mexican-Americans who are experiencing the same kind of discrimination problems which Negroes have experienced in the South." Greenberg said he was certain that "Mexican Americans have employment discrimination problems." The LDF, Greenberg said, had been filing several federal lawsuits regarding employment discrimination. This office has been the major source of most suits.

32. Garcia would go on to win a seat in the state legislature, where he served from 1973 until his death in October 1983. From the Legislative Reference Library of Texas, http://www.lrl.state.tx.us/legeLeaders/members/memberDisplay.cfm?memberID=%20453#terms.

33. Greenberg supports Matt Garcia's assessment of full coffers. He writes (*Crusaders in the Court*, 367) that the LDF's income at the end of 1961 was $586,421; it was $636,000 at the end of 1962, and was $925,000 in August of 1963. And in 1965, it was over $1.7 million.

34. Tijerina, interview.

35. Greenberg, *Crusaders in the Court*, 489. The LDF also tried to help create an organization to support Native American rights but found those matters complicated by issues of tribal treaty rights. He became aware that there were vast differences "among the 263 continual tribes, bands, villages and pueblos and in 300 Alaskan communities." He found it more difficult to apply international law to American issues than to apply the LDF brand to foreign countries. "We did better exporting the idea of American rights to other lands. The Warren Court was an inspiration all over the world. Because of the LDF role in that constitutional revolution human rights groups invited me to go on missions abroad." *Crusaders in the Court*, 490. Greenberg and his

wife, Deborah (Cole) Greenberg, also an LDF attorney, would take their expertise into the international arena by providing various levels of support to sufferers in the Soviet Union, helping Soviet Jews, South Africans, and Filipinos (490–496). Greenberg, *Crusaders in the Court*, 496–498.

36. Greenberg, interview.

37. Tijerina, interview. Information about Padilla's city council tenure is from the San Antonio City Clerk's office of municipal archives and records, http://www.san antonio.gov/clerk/Archives/officials2.aspx.

38. Tijerina recalled that Padilla would caution against being too public in drawing attention to the plight of Mexican Americans, preferring to work behind the scenes. But in this meeting, Padilla, too, was open about the discrimination.

39. The irony is that Greenberg chose La Fonda, a South American restaurant, when he couldn't find a Mexican restaurant near his office. "[It] was about as close to Mexican food as we could get," he said with some amusement years later during an interview.

40. That $6,000 to write the proposal came from the Field Foundation of New York. Tijerina was mistaken in the interview, believing it was the Milton Foundation. But the records of the Field Foundation, held at the Briscoe Center for American History at the University of Texas at Austin, are clear.

41. Tijerina interview.

42. Ibid.

43. Carlos Cadena, transcript from audiotape interview by Sheree Scarborough, San Antonio, Texas, April 23, 1999, Texas Bar Foundation, Tarleton Law Library, University of Texas at Austin. Of course, Cadena was discounting the activists in LULAC circles, including Tijerina. Still, his comments reveal the image many had of LULAC.

44. Greenberg, *Crusaders in the Court*, 478.

45. Tom Seppy, "Court Says Legal Defense Fund Can Use NAACP Initials," *Associated Press*, Jan. 25, 1985. LexisNexis Academic database.

46. Albert Armendariz, videotape interview by Maggie Rivas-Rodriguez, El Paso, Texas, March 10, 2001, Voces Oral History Project, Nettie Lee Benson Latin American Collection, University of Texas Libraries.

47. The use of the identifier "Hispano" by New Mexicans has been the subject of several studies. One of the most exacting analyses is by John M. Nieto-Phillips, *The Language of Blood: The Making of Spanish-American Identity in New Mexico, 1880s-1930s* (Albuquerque: University of New Mexico Press, 2004). Nieto-Phillips writes that Mexican Americans outside of New Mexico have been critical of New Mexicans, accusing them of claiming *hispanidad* as a way of asserting whiteness, thereby establishing American citizenship. But Nieto-Phillips writes that "in the hands of Nuevomexicano politicians, historians, and educators, this heritage served as a rhetorical tool for resistance to further marginalization. When Nuevomexicanos elaborated and deployed their hispanidad, or Spanishness—when they became authors of their own past, authorities of their own language—they often did so as a way of resisting and not accommodating Anglos' ascendancy and touristic fantasies. . . .

[T]he Spanish heritage was both the object of Anglos' fascination and a source of ethnic agency as Nuevomexicanos (of various echelons) struggled to reclaim some degree of control over their political destiny and cultural assets" (8).

48. Sillas was a young lawyer at the time. In 1968 he defended Sal Castro, the high school teacher who led student walkouts in Los Angeles to protest discrimination at their schools. For a full account of the East LA protests, see Mario T. García and Sal Castro, *Blowout!: Sal Castro and the Chicano Struggle for Educational Justice* (Chapel Hill: University of North Carolina Press, 2011).

49. Tijerina, interview. The issue of Mexican American intrastate distrust—particularly between Californios and Tejanos—would make a fascinating study. In interviews with WWII veterans, California veterans often characterize Texas Mexican Americans as less educated and more "country." Texas veterans often say their California counterparts were more assimilated and often spoke no Spanish. Although there were friendships established, members of each group initially were suspicious of one another.

50. Suzanne E. Siegal to Cesar Chavez, Jan. 28, 1970, MALDEF Records, Box 2, Folder 5, Record Group 1, Dept. of Special Collections, Stanford University Libraries. In this letter, a Ford Foundation officer reassured him that MALDEF's fund-raising would "not conflict with that of the United Farm Workers Organizing Committee. May I also point out the fact that the educational of the MALDEF direct mail is very important for, at no cost to anyone but MALDEF, it can bring into one million Mexican American homes this year a new awareness of the Mexican American problem in general."

51. Bernal received his PhD in education from the University of Texas at Austin.

52. The board also named Herman Sillas of Los Angeles, first vice president; Robert Gonzales of San Francisco, second vice president; Manuel H. Garcia, of Tucson, third vice president; and Andres Maldonado as secretary-treasurer. Seven of the directors were nominated to serve for two years: Carlos Cadena; Pete Tijerina; Albert A. Peña, San Antonio attorney; Richard Ibañez, Los Angeles attorney; Jack Greenberg, New York attorney; Albert Armendariz, El Paso attorney; and Dan Sosa, Las Cruces, N.M., attorney. Eight others were also nominated to serve for one-year terms: Levi Martinez of Pueblo, Colo.; Louis Garcia, of San Francisco; Manuel H. Garcia; Sen. Joe Bernal (D-TX); Gregory Luna of San Antonio; Robert Gonzales, of San Francisco; Frank Muñoz of La Puente, Calif.; and Herman Sillas, of Los Angeles. Senator Bernal was the only nonattorney on the board.

53. Joe J. Bernal to Richard A. Ibañez, May 22, 1975, Richard I. Ibañez Papers, Box 2, MALDEF Texas Folder, Dept. of Special Collections, Stanford University Libraries.

54. For a full discussion of this, see the introduction of this volume.

55. Dwight Macdonald, *The Ford Foundation: The Men and the Millions* (New York: Reynal, 1956). Macdonald writes that the heirs would have had to sell most of their shares just to pay the taxes (42–43).

56. Ibid., 42.

57. Richard Magat, *The Ford Foundation at Work: Philanthropic Choices, Methods, and Styles* (New York: Plenum, 1979), 80–81. Magat notes that the Ford Foundation has sought to promote social change, to a point. "If the results of foundation-influenced social change are sufficiently spectacular, they may invite attention and reaction against the program that stimulated them and, to an extent, against foundations themselves. Voter education is a case in point, the Tax Reform Act of 1969 included explicit limitations on the use of tax-exempt funds for this purpose; it is fairly certain that these restrictions were instituted initially because congressional consciousness had been raised by the support that several foundations had given to voter registration programs in the South. A $65,000 grant made by the Foundation to a voter education and registration program confined to the black areas of Cleveland was seized on later as a 'bad case' to which remedial legislative drafting was addressed. Here was an instance of our employing an insensitive means to a good end," 81–82.

58. Macdonald, *The Ford Foundation*, 5.

59. Ibid., 27. In a report after the first probe—called the Cox Report after its chairman, Eugene Cox—the committee said (28–29) there was no evidence that the foundations had sought to "weaken, undermine or discredit the American system of free enterprise . . . while at the same time extolling the virtues of the Socialist state. . . . Many of our citizens confuse the term 'social,' as applied to the discipline of the social sciences, with the term 'Socialism.'" The second report, named for its chairman, Brazilla Carroll Reece, and released in December 1954, found scant evidence of activities supporting Communism. "'However, some of the larger foundations have directly supported 'subversion' in the true meaning of that term—namely, the process of undermining some of our vitally protective concepts and principles. They have actively supported attacks upon our social and governmental system and financed the promotion of Socialism and collective ideas.' As 'subversion' means undermining 'protective'—or G.O.P.–principles, so 'Socialism' means the economic policies of Roosevelt and Truman." Macdonald, *Ford Foundation*, quoting the report, 33–34.

60. According to the Foundation Center, accessed at http://foundationcenter .org/getstarted/onlinebooks/ff/author.html, the Tax Reform Act of 1969 set minimums for how much a private foundation must distribute and created new rules regulating relationships between donors, foundation staff, and board members. The new law also required foundations to file annual reports with the IRS (Form 990-AR and 990-PF) and to make the forms available for inspection by the public. (Beginning in 1982, foundations have been required to file only one form, a revised Form 990-PF.) David Montejano writes that Henry B. Gonzalez also met with Patman. See Montejano, *Quixote's Soldiers: A Local History of the Chicano Movement, 1966–1981*, 108.

61. Leo Grebler, Joan W. Moore, and Ralph C. Guzman, *The Mexican American People: The Nation's Second Largest Minority* (New York: Free Press, 1971).

62. Joan Moore, "Latina/o Studies: The Continuing Need for New Paradigms," *JSRI Occasional Paper* 29, Julian Samora Research Institute (East Lansing: Michigan State University, 1997): 1. Moore goes on to say that when she and the other researchers

gathered the bibliography on Mexican Americans in 1966, there were "no more than a dozen books by and for sociologists about Mexican-Americans published by mainstream academic presses prior to 1965." The few books that had been published were on rural Mexican Americans, she said. Puerto Ricans, because they had settled in large urban areas like Chicago and New York, had received a bit more attention from sociologists. "However, because Latinas/os were so heavily out-numbered in those cities by African-Americans and European ethnics, they tended to be overlooked," 1.

63. This information is from a memorial by the University of California (System) Academic Senate, the University of California, 1988. It can be read at: http://bit .ly/1d3PQl3.

64. Norval D. Glenn, "Some Reflections on a Landmark Publication and the Literature on Mexican Americans," *Social Science Quarterly* 52, no. 1 (June 1971): 8–9. Glenn acknowledged the long-standing neglect of Mexican Americans: between 1966 and 1970, "the three leading sociological journals—the *American Sociological Review*, the *American Journal of Sociology*, and *Social Forces*—[there were] only two articles dealing with Chicanos . . . compared with 38 papers dealing with blacks in the United States" (8). Glenn said there was a similar lack of attention in other general sociological journals: "*Phylon*, a journal devoted to 'race and culture,' published 74 papers on blacks but only two on Mexican Americans. The *Social Studies Quarterly*, with an editorial policy favoring topics related to policy and social issues, received only three manuscripts on Mexican Americans worthy of publication, compared to 48 on blacks. . . . [O]nly *Sociology and Social Research*, which is published in Southern California, contained as many articles on Chicanos as on blacks—five on the former and four on the latter."

65. Ibid. Glenn writes: "Until more Chicanos are recruited into the social sciences, there is likely to be a continuation, and perhaps an intensification, of the recently appearing tension between some Chicano activists and Anglo social scientists who study Chicanos" (10).

66. Jesús Chavarría, "Professor Grebler's Book: The 'Magnum Opus' of a Dying Era of Scholarship," *Social Science Quarterly* 52, no. 1 (June 1971): 11, 12.

67. Ibid., 13.

68. Ibid.

69. Anonymous, "Engaging the Levers and Resources of Power," University of California, Berkeley, School of Social Welfare, http://socialwelfare.berkeley.edu/Stories /hgallegos_story.php. Gallegos went on to form with Luz Vega-Marquis and Elisa Arevalo the group Hispanics in Philanthropy in 1983, dedicated to helping Latino organizations secure grant funding, as well as diversifying boards and staffs.

70. Greenberg, *Crusaders in the Courts*, 371–372. Greenberg writes that he had developed NORI, working with Ford program officials, as an LDF subsidiary—to make funding more palatable to Ford. "NORI wouldn't have the image of a controversial, black civil rights organization. It would attempt to aid the poor in much the same way we were making law on behalf of blacks. If blacks benefited disproportionately from

its programs it would only be because blacks in America made up a disproportionate percentage of the poor and Ford would be spared having to make grants to the contentious civil rights movement." Henry T. Heald, as the Ford Foundation president, was seen as opposing funding the civil rights programs. But when he stepped down, and was replaced by McGeorge Bundy, funding directly to the LDF became possible. The initial check for the initial donation had been made payable to the LDF, and later stipends were intended to be paid to NORI. But the change in leadership allowed the entire amount to be given to the LDF. "We allowed NORI to fade away as a formal organization and the entire grant went to LDF" (372).

71. Ibid., 487.

72. Ylvisaker left the Ford Foundation in 1966, but his interest in disadvantaged groups, including Mexican Americans, was shared by his successor, S. Michael Miller, according to Nicolau and Santiestevan.

73. Ernesto Galarza to S. M. Miller, Sept. 8, 1967, MALDEF Records, PA 06800248, Ford Foundation Archives.

74. Ibid.

75. S. M. Miller to William Pincus, Sept. 13, 1967, MALDEF Records, PA 06800248, Ford Foundation Archives.

76. Pete Tijerina to William Pincus, Aug. 15, 1967, MALDEF Records, PA 06800248, Ford Foundation Archives.

77. Siobhan O. Nicolau and Henry Santiestevan, "Looking Back: A Grantee-Grantor View of the Early Years of the Council of La Raza," in *Hispanics and the Non-Profit Sector*, ed. Herman E. Gallegos and Michael O'Neill (New York: The Foundation Center, 1991), 50.

78. Ibid.

79. Ibid., 51.

80. Ibid., 51–52.

81. Pete Tijerina to William Pincus, Aug. 15, 1967, MALDEF Records, PA 06800248, Ford Foundation Archives.

82. William Pincus to Pete Tijerina, Aug. 23, 1967, MALDEF Records, PA 06800248, Ford Foundation Archives.

83. Pete Tijerina to William Pincus, Aug. 28, 1967, MALDEF Records, PA 06800248, Ford Foundation Archives.

84. "By-laws of Mexican-American Legal Defense and Educational Fund," 1968.

85. MALDEF Draft Proposal to the Ford Foundation, Aug. 7, 1967, MALDEF Records, PA 06800248, Ford Foundation Archives.

86. Ibid., 8.

87. Ibid., 17. "An illustration is the above mentioned case involving Reies Tijerina. Despite widespread sympathy for his cause among Mexican-Americans in New Mexico and Colorado, no money was available for his defense. Attorneys were appointed by the court."

88. Pincus is identified as a program officer in the foundation's 1968 Annual Report. The report notes the foundation had provided grants to "two major efforts by

Mexican-Americans, an ethnic group beset with problems of poverty, immigration, language and discrimination." Those two groups were MALDEF and the Southwest Council of La Raza.

89. Tijerina, interview.

90. Howard R. Dressner to Carlos C. Cadena, April 24, 1968, MALDEF Records, Box 1, Folder 1, Record Group 3, Dept. of Special Collection, Stanford University Libraries.

91. Ibid., 7.

92. Ford Foundation Press Release, May 1, 1968, 1, Richard Ibañez Papers, Box 1, Folder 1; Ibañez, Richard Ibañez Papers, Box 1, Folder 1.

93. Ibid., 1–2.

94. Ibid., 2.

95. Ibid., 5.

96. Ibid.

97. Tijerina, interview.

98. "By-laws of Mexican-American Legal Defense and Educational Fund." Board members present included Judge Carlos C. Cadena; Thomas Guardia Jr.; Dr. Gregory Luna; Andres Maldonado; Father Henry Casso; Father Miguel Barragan (Bishop's Committee for the Spanish-Speaking, San Antonio); Juan Rocha; Pete Tijerina. Present by proxy: Manuel H. Garcia; Albert Armendariz; Levi Martinez (Pueblo, Colo.); Jack Greenberg; Herman Sillas Jr.; Joseph Herrera; Louis Garcia. Letters from other prospective directors are also included with the minutes, but their names are not reflected either as present, or having provided a proxy. These include Kenneth A. Martyn (Vice President for Academic Affairs of California State College at Los Angeles); Robert E. Gonzales (attorney, San Francisco); Richard A. Ibañez (attorney, Los Angeles); Charles S. Vigil (attorney, Denver); Julian Samora (professor, Notre Dame University); George Sanchez (professor, University of Texas at Austin).

99. *The Kerner Report: The 1968 Report of the National Advisory Commission on Civil Disorders*, intro. Tom Wicker (New York: Pantheon, 1988), 233–234.

100. See Susan Ferriss, Ricardo Sandoval, and Diana Hembree, *The Fight in the Fields: Cesar Chavez and the Farmworkers Movement* (New York: Harcourt Brace, 1997).

101. Rodolfo Acuña, *Occupied America: A History of Chicanos*, 7th ed. (New York: Pearson Longman, 2011), 308, 309. At the 1969 conference, participants wrote *El Plan Espiritual de Aztlán*, which Acuña describes (308) as promulgating "the term *Chicano* as a symbol of resistence."

102. Acuña, *Occupied America*, 305–306. The fact of Reies Lopez Tijerina seeking MALDEF's assistance is from letters from Pete Tijerina to the Field Foundation, Aug. 16, 1968, at the Briscoe Center for American History, University of Texas.

103. Armando Navarro, *Mexican American Youth Organization: Avant-Garde of the Chicano Movement in Texas* (Austin: University of Texas Press, 1995), 80, 81.

104. José Ángel Gutiérrez, *The Making of a Chicano Militant: Lessons from Cristal*, Wisconsin Studies in Autobiography (Madison: University of Wisconsin Press, 1998),

100. Another analysis of the work and contributions of MAYO is Navarro, *Mexican American Youth Organization.*

105. Gutiérrez, *The Making of a Chicano Militant*, 101–102.

106. Ibid, 117.

107. For another example, immediately after the war, see Maggie Rivas-Rodriguez, "Framing Racism: Newspaper Coverage of the Three Rivers Incident," in *Mexican Americans and World War II*, ed. Maggie Rivas-Rodriguez (Austin: University of Texas Press, 2005), chap. 8. During the 1949 incident that this chapter discusses, white business leaders and local newspapers in Texas argued that the small town of Three Rivers, Texas, had no racial divisions. National public attention focused on Three Rivers after the local funeral home director denied the use of the funeral parlor to the widow of a Mexican American serviceman killed in the closing days of the war. The American G.I. Forum's Hector P. Garcia came to the widow's aid, and national press criticized Three Rivers and the state of Texas for disrespecting the fallen American soldier and his family—because of their ethnicity. Many civic leaders in Three Rivers continued to deny racial problems. The junior senator from Texas, Lyndon Baines Johnson, intervened, and the remains of Private Felix Longoria were buried at Arlington National Cemetery.

108. "Apologize or Resign, Officers of GI Forum Urge McAllister," *San Antonio Express*, July 9, 1970, 1, 4.

109. James McCrory, "Smith Shaken by S.A. Meeting," *San Antonio Express*, August 28, 1970, 15A.

110. Harold Green to Mario Obledo, April 21, 1970, MALDEF Records, Ford Foundation Archives.

111. Robert Montemayor, telephone interview by Maggie Rivas-Rodriguez, January 29, 2014, Voces Oral History Project.

112. MALDEF Conferences, MALDEF Records, Box 1, Folder 1, Records Group 1, Dept. of Special Collections, Stanford University Libraries; Mario Obledo to Pete Tijerina, 1968, MALDEF Archives.

113. Ibid.

114. George I. Sanchez to Pete Tijerina, Austin, Texas, 1968, George I. Sanchez Papers, Box 25, Folder 1, Nettie Lee Benson Latin American Collection, University of Texas Libraries. Tijerina wrote back, trying to pacify Sanchez: "I have a burden to discharge by way of personal commitments." Ford had recommended working closely with the Inc. Fund. More research into Mexican American educational disparities were needed. "Please try to reconsider as I know that you can contribute greatly to the conference and help us get these people to make additional research if necessary, which would be available at no cost to our Fund."

115. "MALDEF Conferences" (1968–1969); Pete Tijerina to George I. Sanchez, Sept. 30, 1968, George I. Sanchez Papers, Box 25, Folder 1, Nettie Lee Benson Latin American Collection, University of Texas Libraries.

116. "Mario Obledo to MALDEF Board of Directors" (March 4, 1970), 8, MALDEF Records, Record Group 1, Box 2, Folder 6, Special Collections Dept., Stanford University Libraries.

117. Gregory Luna by José Ángel Gutiérrez, Nov. 23, 1968, Oral History Interview, CMAS 4, Special Collections, University of Texas at Arlington Libraries.

118. Mario Obledo to MALDEF Board of Directors, MALDEF Records, Box 2, Folder 6, Record Group 1, Dept. of Special Collections, Stanford University Libraries.

119. Pete Tijerina to Leslie W. Dunbar, Aug. 16, 1968, Box 10, File: MALDEF, Fall 1969-#2, Field Foundation Archives, 1940–1994, Dolph Briscoe Center for American History, University of Texas at Austin.

120. HS to Leslie W. Dunbar, Sept. 20, 1968, Box 10, File: MALDEF, Fall 1969-#2, Field Foundation Archives, 1940–1994, Dolph Briscoe Center for American History, University of Texas at Austin. HS uses the acronym "MALD," and that acronym is seen in the early years in correspondence and even on stationery.

121. Leslie W. Dunbar to Pete Tijerina, Oct. 9, 1968, Box 10, File: MALDEF, Fall 1969-#2, Field Foundation Archives, Dolph Briscoe Center for American History, University of Texas at Austin.

122. Memo to Field Foundation Board of Directors, 1968, Box 10, File: MALDEF, Fall 1969-#2, Field Foundation Archives, 1940–1994, Dolph Briscoe Center for American History, University of Texas at Austin.

123. Leslie Dunbar to Pete Tijerina, Nov. 27, 1968, Field Foundation Archives, Dolph Briscoe Center for American History, University of Texas at Austin.

124. Montejano, *Quixote's Soldiers*, 61.

125. Ibid. Montejano writes that MAUC and MAYO worked with other Chicano organizations and created several other organizations to serve different purposes: the Committee for Barrio Betterment (CBB); El Barrio Unido; the Mexican American Neighborhood Community Organization (MANCO); La Universidad del Barrio (LUB).

126. "Foundation Admits Error," *San Antonio Light*, November 8, 1969, 12.

127. James McCrory, "MAYO Jefe Raps 'Gringo' Policies," *San Antonio Express*, April 11, 1969, 8F.

128. Henry B. Gonzalez to Herman Gallegos, Sept. 10, 1969, Henry B. Gonzalez Papers, Box 2004-127-394, File: Southwest Council of La Raza, 1969, Dolph Briscoe Center for American History, University of Texas at Austin.

129. José Ángel Gutiérrez, "*La Raza* and Revolution: The Empirical Conditions of Revolution in Four South Texas Counties" (master's thesis, St. Mary's University, 1968), 76. Gutiérrez's thesis is in the Henry B. Gonzalez papers. Several passages, particularly where Gutiérrez predicts a revolt, are underlined in red ink. It is unclear whether it was actually Gonzalez who read and made notations to Gutiérrez's work.

130. Ibid., 4.

131. Representative Henry Gonzalez, speaking on "'The Hate Issue,'" 91st Cong., 1st sess., April 22, 1969 (Washington, D.C.: Congressional Record-H 2928–2930, 1969).

132. Montejano, *Quixote's Soldiers*, 108. A critical study of Gonzalez's actions, relations with, and motivations regarding the Mexican American civil rights movement in the 1960s and 1970s would find a ready audience.

133. Navarro, *Mexican American Youth Organization*, 198. The quotation is from Gutiérrez's diary.

134. Henry B. Gonzalez to John R. Silber, April 24, 1969, Henry B. Gonzalez Papers, Box 2004-127/92, Personal Correspondence, 1969, file 4 of 4, Dolph Briscoe Center for American History, University of Texas Archives.

135. W. Gordon Whaley to Henry B. Gonzalez, May 13, 1969, Henry B. Gonzalez Papers, Box 2004-127/92, Personal Correspondence, Dolph Briscoe Center for American History, University of Texas Archives.

136. Joseph M. Montoya, Edward R. Roybal, and Vicenter T. Ximenes to McGeorge Bundy, Jan. 19, 1970, Bernal Papers, Box 56, Folder 1, Nettie Lee Benson Latin American Collection, University of Texas Libraries.

137. "Gonzalez Held Out-Dated," *San Antonio Express*, May 6, 1969, 16A.

138. "A Letter from the Ford Foundation," *Carta Editorial Newsletter*, June-July 1969, 2–4, Henry B. Gonzalez Papers, Box 127/64, MAYO 1969, Dolph Briscoe Center for American History, University of Texas Archives.

139. Henry B. Gonzalez to O. J. Valdez, May 8, 1967, Henry B. Gonzalez Papers, Box 127/394, LULAC 1967, Dolph Briscoe Center for American History, University of Texas Archives.

140. MALDEF brochure, n.d., MALDEF Records, Box 2, Folder 7, Record Group 1.

141. Pete Tijerina to the Ford Foundation, April 21, 1970, MALDEF Records, PA 6800248, Ford Foundation Archives.

142. Ibid., 3.

143. Pete Tijerina to Christopher Edley, April 24, 1970, MALDEF Records, Ford Foundation Archives.

144. Leonard E. Ryan to Pete Tijerina, 1970, MALDEF Records, Ford Foundation Archives.

145. La Raza National Law Students Association to MALDEF Board of Directors, 1970. Although the memo itself is undated, there is a handwritten notation in the upper-left-hand corner of the first page: "Received AM/SP 7/24/70." MALDEF Records, Box 2, Folder 10, Record Group 1, Dept. of Special Collections, Stanford University Libraries.

146. Ibid.

147. Louis Garcia to Albert Armendariz, July 22, 1970, MALDEF Records, Box 2, Folder 10, Record Group 1, Dept. of Special Collections, Stanford University Libraries.

148. Richard A. Ibañez to Albert Armendariz, July 24, 1970, MALDEF Records, Box 2, Folder 10, Record Group 1, Dept. of Special Collections, Stanford University Libraries.

149. Albert Armendariz to MALDEF board, July 27, 1970, MALDEF Records, Box 2, Folder 10, Record Group 1, Dept. of Special Collections, Stanford University Libraries.

150. Leonard E. Ryan to Pete Tijerina, March 13, 1970, MALDEF Records, Box 2, Folder 4, Record Group 1, Dept. of Special Collections, Stanford University Libraries. The three reviewers were William Pincus, formerly a Ford Foundation program officer who had been named president of the Council on Legal Education for Professional Responsibility; Clifford Campbell, of Portland, a consultant for Ford; and Charles Steward, a consultant for the foundation's comptroller's office.

151. Minutes, MALDEF Board Meeting, 1970, MALDEF Records, Box 2, Folder 4, Record Group 1, Dept. of Special Collections, Stanford University Libraries.

152. Edley's title, according to the 1970 Ford Foundation Annual Report. According to minutes from the meeting, the other two Ford Foundation officers present were program officer Leonard E. Ryan and Clifford J. Campbell, a consultant to Ford.

153. Ibid.

154. Ed Castillo, "Maldef Eyes Ultimatum," *San Antonio Light*, March 18, 1970, 65.

155. Minutes, MALDEF Board Meeting, 1970.

156. Castillo, "MALDEF Eyes Ultimatum," 65.

157. Kemper Diehl, "HBG Denies Role in MALD Center Move Plan," *San Antonio News*, March 18, 1970, 1A. For a more complete and lively description and analysis of the divide between Congressman Gonzalez and the leadership of MAYO, MALDEF, and MAUC, see Montejano, *Quixote's Soldiers*.

158. Alice Murphy, "Pete Tijerina Firing Requested by Ford," *San Antonio Express*, March 21, 1970, 1.

159. Ibid.

160. Pete Tijerina to Albert Armendariz, n.d., MALDEF Records, Ford Foundation Archives. Although the letter is undated, it was evidently written in April 1970, as Richard A. Ibañez wrote on April 20, 1970, that he had received the resignation that morning.

161. Richard A. Ibañez to Pete Tijerina, April 20, 1970, MALDEF Records, PA 06800248, Ford Foundation Archives.

162. Greenberg, *Crusaders in the Courts*, 487.

163. MALDEF Annual Report, 1971, MALDEF Records, PA 06800248, Ford Foundation Archives.

164. Herman Sillas to Leonard Ryan, Feb. 10, 1971, MALDEF Records, PA 0680 0248, Ford Foundation Archives.

165. Ibid.

166. Paul Brest to Leonard Ryan, Sept. 1, 1971, MALDEF Records, PA 0680028, Ford Foundation Archives.

167. Ibid.

168. Ibid.

169. Ibid.

170. Ibid.

171. Mario Obledo to McGeorge Bundy, March 22, 1971, MALDEF Records, PA 0680028, Ford Foundation Archives.

172. Vilma S. Martinez to David Ramage, July 23, 1975, Richard A. Ibañez Papers, Box 1, Folder: Program and Planning, Dept. of Special Collections, Stanford University Libraries.

173. Obledo to Bundy, March 22, 1971.

174. Ibid.

175. Ibid.

176. Ibid.

177. Pew Hispanic Center, "Statistical Portrait of Hispanics in the United States; Table 6. Detailed Hispanic Origin: 2009," http://pewhispanic.org/files/factsheets/hispanics2009/Table%206.pdf. Mexican origin people make up 65.5 percent of all U.S. Hispanics, followed by Puerto Ricans with 9.1 percent, Salvadorans with 3.6 percent, and Cubans with 3.5 percent.

178. Jeffrey S. Passal and D'Vera Cohn, *U.S. Population Projections: 2005–2050* (Washington, D.C.: Pew Hispanic Center, 2008).

179. Bernal to Richard A. Ibañez, Richard A. Ibañez Papers, Box 2, Folder: MALDEF Texas, Dept. of Special Collections, Stanford University Libraries.

CONCLUSION: OF ORAL HISTORY AND RESEARCH POSSIBILITIES

1. Victoria-María MacDonald and Benjamin Polk Hoffman, "'Compromising La Causa?': The Ford Foundation and Chicano Intellectual Nationalism in the Creation of Chicano History, 1963–1977," *History of Education Quarterly* 52, no. 2 (May 2012): 281.

2. The following are just a few: Mario T. García, a history professor at UC–Santa Barbara; José Ángel Gutiérrez, at the University of Texas at Arlington; Roberto Trujillo, librarian/archivist at Stanford University; Margo Gutierrez at the Nettie Lee Benson Latin American Collection at the University of Texas at Austin. Others have been doing this for much longer: Thomas H. Kreneck, first at the Metropolitan Library of the Houston Public Library and later at Texas A&M University, Corpus Christi.

3. Juan Gómez-Quiñones, "Toward a Perspective of Chicano History," *Aztlán: A Journal of Chicano Studies* 2, no. 2 (Fall 1971). Gómez-Quiñones calls oral history testimony an "indispensable source," adding, "These are of obvious importance in instances where written testimony is limited." He writes that many historians have been critical of oral histories because "too often, persons with more enthusiasm than training have recorded interviews without context, clear method, or standardized questionnaires, and have uncritically offered and accepted the results as 'documents'" (38).

4. Mario T. García, *The Making of a Mexican American Mayor: Raymond L. Telles of El Paso* (El Paso, Tex.: Texas Western Press, 1998), 20.

5. This is addressed more fully in chapter 3 of this book.

6. Tijerina, interview. The issue of Mexican American intrastate distrust—particularly between Californios and Tejanos—would make a fascinating study. In interviews with WWII veterans, California veterans often characterize Texas Mexican Americans as less educated and less sophisticated. Texas veterans often say their California counterparts were more assimilated and often spoke no Spanish. Although there were friendships established, members of each group were initially suspicious of one another.

7. Ramón Rivas, videotape interview by Maggie Rivas-Rodriguez, San Antonio, Texas, June 12, 1999, Voces Oral History Project, Nettie Lee Benson Latin American Collection, University of Texas Libraries.

8. Ford Foundation Press Release, May 1, 1968, Richard Ibañez Papers, Box 1, Ibañez Folder, Dept. of Special Collections, Stanford University Libraries.

9. Leon Eguía, videotape interview by Liliana Velasquez, Houston, Texas, March 2, 2002, Voces Oral History Project, Nettie Lee Benson Latin American Collection, University of Texas Libraries.

10. Leo Cardenas, "MALDF Makes Legal Fight for Chicanos' Rights," *San Antonio Express*, April 17, 1969, 4. It bears repeating that in its earlier years, MALDEF was often cited by the acronym "MALD" and the initials "MALDF."

11. The 2006 immigration marches, protesting draconian anti-immigrant proposals, were the largest public demonstrations in the history of the country. A few conservative critics characterized them as un-American. But they were mostly described in positive terms.

Selected Bibliography

PUBLISHED SOURCES

Acuña, Rodolfo. *Occupied America: A History of Chicanos*. 7th ed. Boston: Longman, 2011.

Alcalá, Carlos, and Jorge Rangel. "Project Report: De Jure Segregation of Chicanos in Texas Schools." *Harvard Civil Rights-Civil Liberties Review* 7, no. 2 (March 1973): 307–391.

Allsup, Vernon Carl. *The American G.I. Forum: Origins and Evolution*. Monograph. Austin: Center for Mexican American Studies, distributed by the University of Texas Press, 1982.

Avalanche Job Office. *Alpine Beautiful: The Queen City of West Texas*. Alpine, Tex.: *Avalanche* Job Office, ca. 1909.

Baeza, Abelardo. "La Escuela del Barrio: A History of the Alpine Centennial School: 1936–1969." *Journal of Big Bend Studies* 4 (Jan. 1992): 131–145.

———. "La Escuela Escondida: History of the Morgan School in Alpine, Texas, 1929–1954. *Journal of Big Bend Studies* 6 (Jan. 1994): 85–98.

Barrera, Mario, Carlos Muñoz, and Charles Ornelas. "The Barrio as an Internal Colony." In *La Causa Politica: A Chicano Politics Reader*, edited by F. Chris Garcia, 281–301. Notre Dame, Ind.: University of Notre Dame Press, 1974.

Blanton, Carlos Kevin. *The Strange Career of Bilingual Education in Texas, 1836–1981*. Fronteras Series. College Station: Texas A&M University Press, 2004.

Bobcat, Carrizo Springs annual yearbook, 1954 and 1957.

Burstein, Paul. *Discrimination, Jobs, and Politics: The Struggle for Equal Employment in the United States since the New Deal*. Chicago: University of Chicago Press, 1985.

Carroll, Patrick James. *Felix Longoria's Wake: Bereavement, Racism, and the Rise of Mexican American Activism*. Austin: University of Texas Press, 2003.

Casey, Clifford B. *Alpine, Texas, Then and Now*. Seagraves, Tex.: Pioneer Book Publishers, 1981.

Chavarría, Jesús. "Professor Grebler's Book: The 'Magnum Opus' of a Dying Era of Scholarship." *Social Science Quarterly* 52, no. 1 (June 1, 1971): 11–14.

Converse, Philip E., and Georges Dupeux. "De Gaulle and Eisenhower: The Public Image of the Victorious General." In *Elections and the Political Order*, by Angus Campbell, Philip E. Converse, Warren E. Miller, and Donald E. Stokes. New York: Wiley, 1966.

Curtin, Mary Ellen. "Reaching for Power: Barbara C. Jordan and Liberals in the Texas Legislature, 1966–1972." *Southwestern Historical Quarterly* 108, no. 2 (Oct. 2004): 210–231.

D'Antonio, William V., and William H. Form. *Influentials in Two Border Cities: A Study in Community Decision-Making*. Notre Dame, Ind.: University of Notre Dame Press, 1965.

DeAnda, James. "Civil Rights—Need for Executive Branch to Take Positive Steps to Rectify Discrimination in Jury Selection, Voting Eligibility and School Enrollment." In *The Mexican American: A New Focus on Opportunity*. Testimony presented at the Cabinet Committee Hearings on Mexican American Affairs, El Paso, Texas, October 26–28, 1967. Washington, D.C.: Inter-Agency Committee on Mexican American Affairs. 1969.

Davis, Michael D., and Hunter R. Clark. *Thurgood Marshall: Warrior at the Bar, Rebel on the Bench*. New York: Carol Publishing Group, 1992.

De la Garza, Rudolph O. "Voting Patterns in 'Bi-Cultural El Paso': a Contextual Analysis of Chicano Voting Behavior." *Aztlán: A Journal of Chicano Studies* 5, nos. 1–2 (1974): 235–260.

Eschbach, Karl, and Maggie Rivas-Rodriguez. "Navigating Bureaucratic Imprecision in the Search for an Accurate Count of Latino/a Military Service in World War II." In *Latina/os and World War II: Mobility, Agency, and Ideology*, edited by Maggie Rivas-Rodriguez and B. V. Olguín, ix–xix. Austin: University of Texas Press, 2014.

Ferriss, Susan, Ricardo Sandoval, and Diana Hembree. *The Fight in the Fields: Cesar Chavez and the Farmworkers Movement*. New York: Harcourt Brace, 1997.

Forbes, Jack B. *Hearing before the Unites States Commission on Civil Rights*. Washington, D.C.: Government Printing Office, 1969, 24–36.

Galarza, Ernesto, *Man of Fire: Selected Writings*. Edited by Armando Ibarra and Rodolfo D. Torres. Urbana: University of Illinois Press, 2014.

Gallegos, Mario. "History of Hispanic Firefighters in Houston." In *Hispanics in Houston and Harris County, 1519–1986: A Sesquicentennial Celebration*, edited by Dorothy F. Caram, Anthony G. Dworkin, and Néstor Rodríguez. Houston: Houston Hispanic Forum, 1989.

García, Mario T. *Desert Immigrants: The Mexicans of El Paso, 1880–1920*. New Haven, Conn.: Yale University Press, 1981.

———. *The Making of a Mexican American Mayor: Raymond L. Telles of El Paso*. El Paso: Texas Western Press, University of Texas at El Paso, 1998.

———. *Mexican Americans: Leadership, Ideology, and Identity, 1930–1960*. New Haven, Conn.: Yale University Press, 1989.

Gómez-Quiñonez, Juan. "Toward a Perspective of Chicano History." *Aztlán* 2, no. 2 (Fall 1971): 1–49.

Gonzales, Phillip B. "*La Junta de Indignación*: Hispano Repertoire of Collective Protest in New Mexico, 1884–1993." *Western Historical Quarterly* 31, no. 2 (Summer 2000): 161–186.

Gonzalez, Henry. Speaking on "The Hate Issue." 91st Congress, 1st sess., April 22, 1969. *Congressional Record* H2929 (1969). Washington, D.C.: Government Printing Office, 1969.

Greenberg, Jack. *Crusaders in the Courts: How a Dedicated Band of Lawyers Fought for the Civil Rights Revolution*. New York: Basic Books, 1994.

Griswold del Castillo, Richard. "La Raza Hispano Americana: The Emergence of an Urban Culture among the Spanish Speaking of Los Angeles, 1850–1880." Master's thesis, UCLA, 1974.

Griswold del Castillo, Richard, and Arnoldo De León. *North to Aztlán: A History of Mexican Americans in the United States*. New York: Twayne, 1996.

Gutiérrez, José Ángel. *The Making of a Chicano Militant: Lessons from Cristal*. Madison: University of Wisconsin Press, 1998.

———. *El Politico: The Mexican American Elected Official*. El Paso, Tex.: Mictla, 1972.

———. "La Raza and Revolution: The Empirical Conditions of Revolution in Four South Texas Counties." Master's thesis, St. Mary's University, 1968.

Hernandez, Alfred J. "Civil Service and the Mexican American." In *The Mexican American: A New Focus on Opportunity, Testimony Presented at the Cabinet Committee Hearings on Mexican American Affairs*. Inter-Agency Committee on Mexican American Affairs, El Paso, Texas, Oct. 26–28, 1967.

Hoogenboom, Ari. "The Pendleton Act and the Civil Service." *The American Historical Review* 64, no. 2 (Jan. 1959): 301–318.

Information and History of the Big Bend-Davis Mountains Area: Issued on the Sixtieth Anniversary of the "Avalanche." Alpine, Tex.: Webb, 1951.

James, Rawn, Jr. *Root and Branch: Charles Hamilton Houston, Thurgood Marshall, and the Struggle to End Segregation*. New York: Bloomsbury, 2010.

Macdonald, Dwight. *The Ford Foundation: The Men and the Millions*. New York: Reynal, 1956.

MacDonald, Victoria-María, and Benjamin Polk Hoffman, "'Compromising La Causa?': The Ford Foundation and Chicano Intellectual Nationalism in the Creation of Chicano History, 1963–1977." *History of Education Quarterly* 52, no. 2 (May 2012): 251–258.

Magat, Richard. *The Ford Foundation at Work: Philanthropic Choices, Methods, and Styles*. New York: Plenum, 1979.

Martinez, Oscar J. *The Chicanos of El Paso: An Assessment of Progress*. El Paso: Texas Western Press, 1980.

McLynn, Frank. *Villa and Zapata: A History of the Mexican Revolution*. New York: Carroll and Graf, 2000.

Montejano, David. *Anglos and Mexicans in the Making of Texas, 1836–1986*. Austin: University of Texas Press, 1987.

———. *Quixote's Soldiers: A Local History of the Chicano Movement, 1966–1981*. Austin: University of Texas Press, 2010.

Navarro, Armando. *The Cristal Experiment: A Chicano Struggle for Community Control*. Madison: University of Wisconsin Press, 1998.

———. *Mexican American Youth Organization: Avant-Garde of the Chicano Movement in Texas*. Austin: University of Texas Press, 1995.

Nicolau, Siobhan O., and Henry Santiestevan. "Looking Back: A Grantee-Grantor View of the Early Years of the Council of La Raza." In *Hispanics and the Non-Profit Sector*, edited by Herman E. Gallegos and Michael O'Neill, 49–66. New York: Foundation Center, 1991.

Nieto-Phillips, John M. *The Language of Blood: The Making of Spanish-American Identity in New Mexico, 1880s–1930s*. Albuquerque: University of New Mexico Press, 2004.

Olivas, Michael A., ed. *"Colored Men" and "Hombres Aquí"*: Hernandez v. Texas *and the Emergence of Mexican-American Lawyering*. Houston: Arte Público, 2006.

———. "Review Essay—the Arc of Triumph and the Agony of Defeat: Mexican Americans and the Law." *Journal of Legal Education* 60, no. 2 (Nov. 2010): 354–368.

Orozco, Cynthia. *No Mexicans, Women, or Dogs Allowed: The Rise of the Mexican American Civil Rights Movement*. Austin: University of Texas Press, 2009.

Overacker, Louise. *Money in Elections*. New York: Macmillan, 1932.

Perales, Alonso S. *En Defensa de Mi Raza*. San Antonio: Artes Gráficas, 1936–1937.

Pycior, Julie Leininger. "La Raza Organizes Mexican American Life in San Antonio, 1915–1930, Reflected in Mutualista Activities." PhD dissertation, University of Notre Dame, 1979.

———. *LBJ and Mexican Americans: The Paradox of Power*. Austin: University of Texas Press, 1997.

Ramirez, José A. *To the Line of Fire!: Mexican Texans and World War I*. C. A. Brannen Series, no. 11. College Station: Texas A&M University Press, 2009.

Ramos, Henry. *The American GI Forum: In Pursuit of the Dream, 1948–1983*. Houston: Arte Público, 1998.

Rivas-Rodriguez, Maggie. "Framing Racism: Newspaper Coverage of the Three Rivers Incident." In *Mexican Americans and World War II*, edited by Maggie Rivas-Rodriguez, 201–220. Austin: University of Texas Press, 2005.

Rubio, Philip F. *There's Always Work at the Post Office*. Chapel Hill: University of North Carolina Press, 2010.

Sáenz, José de la Luz. *Los México-Americanos en la Gran Guerra*. San Antonio: Artes Gráficas, 1933.

———. *The World War I Diary of José de la Luz Sáenz*. C. A. Brannen series. Translated by Emilio Zamora with Ben Maya. College Station: Texas A&M University Press, 2014.

San Miguel, Guadalupe, Jr. "The Struggle against Separate and Unequal Schools:

Middle-Class Mexican Americans and the Desegregation Campaign in Texas, 1929–1957." *History of Education Quarterly* 23, no. 3 (1983).

———. *"Let All of Them Take Heed": Mexican Americans and the Campaign for Educational Equality in Texas, 1910–1981.* Austin: University of Texas Press, 1987.

Schmidt, Benno C., Jr. "Juries, Jurisdiction, and Race Discrimination: The Lost Promise of *Strauder v. West Virginia.*" *Texas Law Review* 61, no. 8 (1983): 1401–1434.

Schneider, James G. *The Navy V12 Program: Leadership for a Lifetime.* Boston: Houghton Mifflin, 1987.

Sears, David O., Jim Sidanius, and Lawrence Bobo. *Racialized Politics: The Debate about Racism in America.* Chicago: University of Chicago Press, 2000.

Stone, Irving. *Clarence Darrow for the Defense: A Biography.* Garden City, N.Y.: Doubleday, Doran, 1941.

Strum, Philippa. Mendez v. Westminster: *School Desegregation and Mexican-American Rights.* Lawrence: University Press of Kansas, 2010.

Teachman, Jay, and Vaughn R. A. Call. "The Effect of Military Service on Educational, Occupational, and Income Attainment." *Social Science Research* 25 (1966): 1–31.

Texas Attorney General's Office. *Digest of Opinions of the Attorney General of Texas.* 1947–1981. Austin: Texas Attorney General's Office, 1942–1982.

Theriault, Sean M. "Patronage, the Pendleton Act, and the Power of the People." *Journal of Politics* 65, no. 1 (Feb. 2003): 50–68.

Timmons, W. H. *El Paso: A Borderlands History.* El Paso: Texas Western Press, 1990.

Tirado, Miguel David. "Mexican American Community Political Organization: 'The Key to Chicano Political Power.'" In *La Causa Política: A Chicano Politics Reader,* edited by F. Chris Garcia, 105–127. Notre Dame, Ind.: University of Notre Dame Press, 1974.

United States Commission on Civil Rights. *Hearing before the United States Commission on Civil Rights, San Antonio, Texas, December 9–14, 1968.* Washington, D.C.: Government Printing Office, 1969.

United States Commission on Civil Rights. *Stranger in One's Land.* Clearinghouse Publication no. 19. Washington, D.C.: Government Printing Office, May 1970.

United States Commission on Civil Rights. Texas Advisory Committee. *Texas, the State of Civil Rights Ten Years Later, 1968–1978: A Report.* Washington, D.C.: Government Printing Office, 1980.

United States National Advisory Commission on Civil Disorders. *The Kerner Report: The 1968 Report of the National Advisory Commission on Civil Disorders.* Introduction by Tom Wicker. New York: Pantheon, 1988.

Weber, David J. *Myth and the History of the Hispanic Southwest: Essays.* Albuquerque: University of New Mexico Press, 1988.

Wilson, Steven Harmon. "Some Are Born White, Some Achieve Whiteness, and Some Have Whiteness Thrust upon Them: Mexican Americans and the Politics of Racial Classification in the Federal Judicial Bureaucracy, Twenty-Five Years after *Hernandez v. Texas.* In *"Colored Mean" and "Hombres Aquí":* Hernandez v. Texas *and the*

Emergence of Mexican American Lawyering, edited by Michael A. Olivas, 123–142. Houston: Arte Público, 2006.

Zamora, Emilio. "Mexico's Wartime Intervention on Behalf of Mexicans in the United States: A Turning of Tables." In *Mexican Americans and World War II*, edited by Maggie Rivas-Rodriguez, 221–243. Austin: University of Texas Press, 2005.

ARCHIVES

Ford Foundation Archives, New York City

MALDEF Records

Stanford University, Special Collections, Stanford, California

MALDEF Records
Richard Ibañez Papers

Texas State Archives

Papers of J. W. Edgar
Records of the Texas Education Agency

University of Texas at Austin, Dolph Briscoe Center for American History

Henry B. Gonzalez Papers
Field Foundation of New York Archives

University of Texas at Austin Libraries, Nettie Lee Benson Latin American Collection

Joe J. Bernal Papers
George I. Sanchez Papers
G.I. Forum Papers

ORAL HISTORY INTERVIEWS

Voces Oral History Project, Nettie Lee Benson Latin American Collection, University of Texas Libraries. (The U.S. Latino & Latina WWII Oral History Project changed its name to the Voces Oral History Project in 2011; all of the interviews are listed under Voces.)

Aguirre, Mike. Interview by Aryn Sedler. Videotape. San Marcos, Texas. March 24, 2000.

Armendariz, Albert. Interview by Maggie Rivas-Rodriguez. Videotape. El Paso, Texas. March 16, 2001.

Bonilla, Freddy. Interview by Maggie Rivas-Rodriguez. Audiotape. El Paso, Texas. August 11, 2011.

Dominguez, Leo. Interview by Maggie Rivas-Rodriguez, Audiotape. Alpine, Texas. August 17, 2012.

Dominguez, Virginia. Interviewed by Maggie Rivas-Rodriguez, Audiotape. Alpine, Texas. August 17, 2012.

Eguía, Leon. Interview by Liliana Velasquez. Videotape. Houston, Texas. March 2, 2002.

Flores, Armando. Interview by Bettina Luis. Videotape. Corpus Christi, Texas. March 24, 2001,

Gallego, Elena, speaking on Pete Gallego's interview. Interview by Maggie Rivas-Rodriguez. Videotape. El Paso, Texas. March 9, 2001.

Gallego, Pete A. Interview by Maggie Rivas-Rodriguez. Videotape. El Paso, Texas. March 9, 2001.

Greenberg, Jack. Interviewed by Maggie Rivas-Rodriguez. Videotape. Manhattan, New York. April 26, 2004.

Hernandez, Alfred J. Interview by Ernest Eguía. Videotape. Houston, Texas. October 24, 2002.

Leyva, Elidia G. Interviewed by Maggie Rivas-Rodriguez. Audiotape. Alpine, Texas. August 17, 2012.

Montemayor, Robert. Interview by Maggie Rivas-Rodriguez. Telephone recording. January 29, 2014.

Pallanez, Mary. Interviewed by Maggie Rivas-Rodriguez. Audiotape. Alpine, Texas. August 17, 2012.

Rivas, Ramón. Interview by Maggie Rivas-Rodriguez. Videotape. San Antonio, Texas. June 12, 1999.

Tijerina, Pete. Interviewed by Maggie Rivas-Rodriguez and Maro Robbins. Videotape. San Antonio, Texas. October 20, 2002.

Uranga, Charles V. Interview by Tony Cantu. Videotape. San Antonio, Texas. January 27, 2001.

Vasquez, Armando. Interview by Maggie Rivas-Rodriguez. Videotape. Marfa, Texas. August 17, 2012.

Walker, Josephine Keller Ledesma. Interviewed by Monica Rivera. Videotape. Austin, Texas. February 17, 2001.

University of Texas at El Paso, Oral History Institute

Telles, Raymond. Interviewed by Oscar J. Martinez. Audiotape. El Paso, Texas. October 22, 1975.

University of Texas at Arlington Libraries

Luna, Gregory. Interviewed by José Ángel Gutierrez. Audiotape. CMAS 4, Special Collections.

Index

Page numbers in italics refer to images.

Perez, Febronia Florian, 16
Perez, Ignacio, 94
Pincus, William, 77, 87, 88, 92, 152n150
Political Association of Spanish-
    speaking Organizations (PASSO),
    5, 6
poll tax: in Crystal City, 5, 6; in El Paso,
    50, 59, 90; as voter suppression, 90,
    125n5, 136n22, 136n23
Pooley, Ed, 52, 136
Port Isabel, 58
Postal Service, 15, 55, 56, 138n47–49
Pravda, 84
Pycior, Julie Leininger, 3, 4

Quiñones, Juan Gomez, 119

Ramirez, Celia Gomez, 13
Rangel, Jorge, 8, 31, 131n49
Raza Unida Party, 6, 127n32
Registration Act of 1966, 90
Rice, Ben H., 32
Rice, Gilbert, 105
"Ring," the, 47
Rio Arriba County Courthouse, 94
Robert E. Lee Hotel, 72
Robstown, 34
Rogers, Tom, 51, 52
Rojo, Alberto, 35–39, *36*, 42
Ronstadt, Linda, 118
Roosevelt, Franklin D., 48
Roybal, Edward, 5, 90, 103, 126n27
Ryan, Leonard, 107, 109, 114

Samora, Julian, 85, 119
San Antonio Public Service Board, 93
Sanchez, George I., 26, *82*, 103, 118;
    and black-brown relations, 143n30;
    as fund-raiser, 28, 83, 142n28; and
    MALDEF, 76, 96, 97, 150n113
San Elizario, 50
San Miguel, Guadalupe, 18, 32
Santiesteban, Tati, 40

Santiestevan, Henry, 87, 88, 148n72
School of the Sacred Heart, 16
SER-Jobs for Progress, 81
Silber, John R., 103
Sillas, Herman, 81, 114, 115, 145n48,
    149n98
Singer, Vilma Martinez. *See* Martinez,
    Vilma
Sixth Amendment, 65
Smith, Preston, 95
Snelson, W. E. "Pete," 40, 41
Social Science Quarterly, 84, 147n64
Sosa, Dan, 81, 111, 145n52
Sotelo, Johnny, 13, 40, 133n78
Southern Pacific Railroad, 15, 46
South Texas College of Law, 72
Southwest Council of La Raza, 87, 101,
    102, 149n88
Sovern, Michael I., 96
St. Mary's University, 72, 94
Student Nonviolent Coordinating Com-
    mittee (SNCC), 79, 93
Sul Ross University, 23, 24, 27, 120; and
    Pete Gallego, 35, 42

Tafolla, Jimmy, 72
Tahoka, 95, 96
Teamsters Union, 5
Telles, Ramón, 47–50
Telles, Raymond L., *49*, 120, 136nn20–21,
    136n23, 136n28; ambassador to Costa
    Rica, 61, 62; election of, 8, 45, 46;
    and family connections, 47, 120; as
    mayor, 54, 59, 61; political campaigns
    of, 50–52, 139n63, 139n66; as World
    War II veteran, x, 48, 49
Telles, Richard, 48, 50, 62, 120
Texas A&M University, ix
Texas Education Agency, 30–32, 38, 39
Texas Farmworker Union, 94
Texas Rangers, 90
Texas State Board of Education, 28–30
Texas Tech University, 95

Tijerina, Graciela Gonzalez, 80
Tijerina, Pete, *70*, 116, 117, 120, 122; as
attorney, 67, 73; and Field Foundation, 98, 99, 144n40; and Ford Foundation, 87–89, 91–93, 109, 110–114,
127; and Jack Greenberg, 77–79; and
José Ángel Gutierrez, 103; and jury
selection, 65, 66; and LULAC Council 2, 67, 73, 86; and MALDEF, 6, 9,
69, 76–81, 96–99, 109, 120, 145n52,
150n113; in New Mexico, 81, 120; and
scholarship program, 106, 107; youth
of, 71, 72
Tijerina, Reies Lopez, 85, 94, 98, 99,
148n87, 149n102
Treaty of Guadalupe Hidalgo, 2, 99

University of California, Berkeley, 90,
96, 108, 147
University of California, Los Angeles
(UCLA), 84, 90
University of Southern California Law
School, 53
University of Texas, ix

University of Texas at El Paso, 53
Uranga, Charlie V., 16
Uranga, Clemente J., 15, 16, 129n14
Urbiñas, Luis, 117
U.S. Commission on Civil Rights, 1, 8,
17, 37
U.S. Department of Justice, 58, 59
U.S. Department of Labor, 56, 59

Valenzuela, Angelita Ramirez, 21, 22
Valenzuela, Francisco, 21, 130n30
Velasquez, Willie, 94
Vidauri, Soledad, 27
Vista program, 96, 97
Viva Kennedy Clubs, 5, 69
V-12 officer-training program, 74

White, Richard, 62
Winn, C. L., 38, 40, 41, 43
Woods, L. A., 31, 131n49

Ximenes, Vincente, 103

Ylvisaker, Paul, 84, 85, 148n72